Exploring
Numbers
with

Python

By

Jack McCabe

Exploring Numbers with Python

ISBN: 9781072202165

Dedication and Appreciation

This publication is dedicated to **Randy Weaver**, a generous friend, who has edited my last three books. Randy has very little interest in my publication topics, yet continues to patiently correct my grammatic blunders.

Doug Blanding, a friend with a design-engineering background, generously took the time to help me become a Python programmer. He has been programming with Python for over twenty years and has made me aware of the richness of the language.

Exploring Numbers with Python

Table of Contents

Preface

Early in 2019, and with the help of a friend, I began learning and using the computer programming language **Python**. I wrote programs to solve number problems, to play games and to explore mathematical discoveries made by ancient mathematicians: men like **Euclid**, **Fermat** and **Gauss**. Their discoveries about numbers were not prompted by any practical use of numbers, rather, they each had a need to ponder and discover hidden properties of numbers. They were rewarded with the thrill and joy of discovery.

Python is not my first experience with computer programming. In the early 70's, while teaching math at Temple University, I learned how to write programs in **FORTRAN**, an earlier programming language used by scientists and engineers. Programming in the 70's were the days of punch-cards and large IBM computers.

Ten years later, while teaching high school math, I purchased a Radio Shack computer. This small desk-top computer included the programming language BASIC. Writing programs in BASIC enabled me to explore some elementary properties of numbers. The computer became my brush, the programs became my oils, while the computer screen became my canvas. I became a happy artist.

In the mid-eighties, after my teaching duties were over, I used **TRUE BASIC** to create computer programs for some commercial customers. Then, as a result of my experience with Advanced Placement Computer Science, I learned to program in **Pascal**.

While learning each new programming language, I increased my skills with logic. Having success with a new program inspired me to explore deeper properties of numbers. To find these deep properties, I turned to books about the history of mathematics. These books revealed the discoveries of **Euclid**, **Fermat**, **Gauss** and other ancient mathematicians. I studied classical algorithms created by these ancient mathematicians and was inspired to create some of my own. Computer programming gave me the opportunity to implement these search procedures and algorithms.

My earlier programs were all procedural, whereas modern programming languages, such as **Java** and **Python**, are object oriented, with objects like strings, lists, tuples and dictionaries. **Python's** richness lies in the fact that it enables the creation of very readable code.

For example, suppose I want to create a list of words from a string of letters. The letters could be in the form of a sentence. Given the sentence 'Men are not created equal.' executing the **Python** code:

```python
sentence = 'Men are not created equal.'
words = []
word = ''
letter = ''
Length = len(sentence)
while Length > 1:
    letter = sentence[0]
    if letter.isalpha():
        word = word + letter
        sentence = sentence.strip(letter)
        Length = Length - 1
    else:
        words.append(word)
        word = ''
        sentence = sentence.strip(letter)
        Length = Length - 1
words.append(word)
print(words)
```

will produce the output:
['Men', 'are', 'not', 'created', 'equal']

A reader can easily follow the intentions of the program. But **Python** provides a more sophisticated solution. The code:

```
sentence = 'Men are not created equal.'
words = sentence.split()
print(words)
```

will produce the same result.

. . .

This book is the result of my learning to write some rather easy **Python** programs. I wrote programs to explore situations where numbers are involved. These situations include number problems, games, dates and discoveries regarding hidden properties of numbers. These hidden properties were discovered centuries ago by ancient mathematicians. I wrote this book to share these **Python** programs as well to reveal some history of mathematics.

. . .

Chapter One: Playing with the Language

1.1 A Fictitious Problem

Professor Smart lives on Long Street, a street where the house-numbers are consecutive numbers, beginning with the number 1. Smart's house-number has two properties:

1 - Smart's house-number is a **three-digit** number.

2 - The sum of the house-numbers **below** Smart's house **equals** the sum of the house-numbers **above** Smart's house.

My challenge is to write a **Python** program to find and confirm Professor Smart's house-number; as well as the number of the last house on his street.

I will need some formulas from arithmetic. The formula $\frac{N(N+1)}{2}$, attributed to Carl Frederick Gauss, provides the sum of the numbers from 1 to N.

For example: the sum of the numbers from 1 to 100 equals $\frac{100(100+1)}{2}$, or 5,050.

A second formula, related to Gauss's formula, will provide the sum of the numbers from N to M. The formula is $\frac{M(M+1)}{2} - \frac{N(N-1)}{2}$.

For example, the sum of the numbers from 100 to 200 equals $\frac{200*201}{2} - \frac{100*99)}{2}$, or $20{,}100 - 4{,}950$, or 15,150.

I need some equations that will lead to a solution of this problem. Letting **H** represent Smart's house-number, the **sum** of the house-numbers **below** his house-number equals the sum of the consecutive numbers from **1 to H-1.** Using Gauss' formula results in the equation $\textbf{\textit{sum below}} = \frac{(H-1)H}{2}$.

Letting **L** represent the house-number of the last house on Smart's street, leads to the equation $\textbf{\textit{sum above}} = \frac{L(L+1)}{2} - \frac{H(H+1)}{2}$.

Combining the two equations leads to the equation $\frac{(H-1)H}{2} = \frac{L(L+1)}{2} - \frac{H(H+1)}{2}$, which leads to the equation $\textbf{2H}^2 = \textbf{L}^2 + \textbf{L.}$ Solving this equation for **H** results in the equation, $\textbf{\textit{H}} = \sqrt{\frac{L^2+L}{2}}$.

I now have a mathematical relationship between **H** and **L**, i.e., between Smart's house-number and the house-number of the last house on Smart's street.

I could use a **trial-and-error** approach to find solutions to the equation $H = \sqrt{\dfrac{L^2 + L}{2}}$. For example, if I substitute 500 for **L** and calculate $H = \sqrt{\dfrac{500^2 + 500}{2}}$, the result will be H = 500.49975, which is not a three-digit number. I will let a **Python** program perform these substitutions.

The smallest possible number for **H** is 100. If there is a solution to the equation $H = \sqrt{\dfrac{L^2 + L}{2}}$, the value of **L** must be between 102 and 999. The **Python** program will perform the search by substituting the numbers 102, 103, 104, etc., until the formula, $H = \sqrt{\dfrac{L^2 + L}{2}}$, yields a **three-digit** number. If these substitutions reach L = 999 without finding a three-digit whole number, then the problem has no answer.

An expression like $\sqrt{\frac{L^2+L}{2}}$ usually results in a decimal number. The program will use this fact to determine if the result of the calculations of $\sqrt{\frac{L^2+L}{2}}$ is a three-digit whole number. To determine if **H** is a three-digit number, the program will apply the 'int' function, known in mathematics as the **greatest-integer** function.

For a decimal number, the 'int' function returns the largest integer less than the decimal number. For example: int(2.0001) = 2, while int(.99999) = 0.

By comparing the value of $\sqrt{\frac{L^2+L}{2}}$ with the **integer-value** of $\sqrt{\frac{L^2+L}{2}}$, the program might find Smart's house-number.

If the program finds Smart's house number and the number of houses on his street, the program will then confirm these solutions. The code for the program is shown on the next page.

"""Professor Smart lives on Long Street, a street where the house-numbers are consecutive numbers, beginning with the number 1. Smart's house-number has two properties:

   1 - Smart's house-number is a three-digit number.
   2 - The sum of the house-numbers below Smart's house
      equals the sum of the house-numbers above Smart's house.

The program, **House_Number**, uses a search procedure to find Smart's house number and the number of houses on Long Street.
"""

```python
# If there is a solution, the program
# should find it before last_house = 1000.
for last_house in range(102, 999):
    house_num = ((last_house**2 + last_house) / 2)**0.5
    if int(house_num) == house_num:
        print('FOUND IT!',)
        break
print ('')
print ('Professor Smart lives at', int(house_num), 'Long Street,')
print ('a street containing', last_house, 'houses.')

# Confirming Smart's house number.

sum_below = int(house_num*(house_num + 1) / 2)
sum_above = int((((last_house + house_num) / 2)*(last_house - house_num + 1)))
print ('The sum of the house-numbers below Smarts house is', sum_below)
print ('The sum of the house-numbers above Smarts house is', sum_above)
```

. . .

Executing the program results in:

FOUND IT!

Smart lives at 204 Long Street,
a street containing 288 houses.
The sum of the house-numbers below Smarts house is 20910
The sum of the house-numbers above Smarts house is 20910

. . .

1.2 Five-Card-Draw

Five-card-draw, is a poker game where the player is dealt five cards and then given an opportunity to improve the hand by discarding some or all of the cards in the hand. Each discarded card is then replaced with a card from the remaining cards in the deck.

A common situation is when the first five cards consist of both two pairs as well as four cards of the same suit. The player will discard one card but must decide between holding the four cards with the same suit, hoping for a flush, versus, holding the two pairs, hoping for a full-house.

The order of values of a hand, along with the probability of the hand is shown below:

Royal Flush	0.0000015
Straight Flush	0.000014
Four of a Kind	0.00024
Full-House	0.0014
Flush	0.0020
Straight	0.0039
Three of a Kind	0.021
Two Pair	0.048
Pair	0.42

A full-house is worth more than a flush, but has a lower probability of occurring (0.0014 versus 0.0020). In a casino where one might find a video version as described above, the pay-off will reflect the varying probability of each final five card hand

.

My challenge is to write a **Python** program enabling one to practice for playing on a video poker machine. The code for the program is shown below and on the next two pages.

```
""" FIVE-CARD-DRAW: The program creates a deck of playing
cards consisting of four suits with 13 cards in each suit.
The player is dealt five cards and can then attempt
to improve the hand by discarding three or less cards
and receiving a replacement for each card discarded.
"""

def pick_a_card():
    n = randint(0, len(deck) - 1)
    card = deck[n]
    if card in deck:
        deck.remove(card)
    return card

def display_hand():
    for j in range(len(hand)):
        card = hand[j]
        print(j + 1, ', card)
```

```
def remove_a_card():
    n = int(input('Enter card number to be removed:'))
    card = hand[n - 1]
    hand.remove(card)
    if card in deck:
        deck.remove(card)
    disply = display_hand()
    return hand

# Main program:
from random import randint

suits = ['DIAMOND', 'CLUB', 'HEART', 'SPADE']
values = ['ACE', 'TWO', 'THREE', 'FOUR', 'FIVE', 'SIX',
'SEVEN', 'EIGHT', 'NINE', 'TEN', 'JACK', 'QUEEN', 'KING']
deck = []
hand = []
hand_converted = []
card = []

for VALUE in values:
    for SUIT in suits:
        pair = [VALUE, SUIT]
        deck.append(pair)

for j in range(1, 6):
    card = pick_a_card()
    hand.append(card)
    hand.sort()

disply = display_hand()
m = int(input('How many cards do you want to discard?: '))
```

```
for j in range(1, m + 1):
    hand = remove_a_card()

for j in range(1, m + 1):
    card = pick_a_card()
    hand.append(card)
    hand.sort()

print('Your final hand')
disply = display_hand()
```

. . .

See several executions of the program below and on the next two pages.

```
1  THREE of SPADE
2  FOUR of HEART
3  FIVE of CLUB
4  SIX of DIAMOND
5  SEVEN of SPADE
How many cards do you want to discard?:0
Your final hand
1  THREE of SPADE
2  FOUR of HEART
3  FIVE of CLUB
4  SIX of DIAMOND
5  SEVEN of SPADE
```

A straight.

1 TWO of DIAMOND
2 FOUR of DIAMOND
3 EIGHT of DIAMOND
4 JACK of HEART
5 KING of HEART
How many cards do you want to discard?:3
Enter card number to be removed:1
1 FOUR of DIAMOND
2 EIGHT of DIAMOND
3 JACK of HEART
4 KING of HEART
Enter card number to be removed:1
1 EIGHT of DIAMOND
2 JACK of HEART
3 KING of HEART
Enter card number to be removed:1
1 JACK of HEART
2 KING of HEART
Your final hand
1 FIVE of SPADE
2 JACK of CLUB
3 JACK of HEART
4 JACK of HEART
5 KING of HEART

Three Jacks.

1 FIVE of DIAMOND
2 FIVE of CLUB
3 SEVEN of DIAMOND
4 SEVEN of CLUB
5 NINE of SPADE
How many cards do you want to discard?:1
Enter card number to be removed:5
1 FIVE of DIAMOND
2 FIVE of CLUB
3 SEVEN of DIAMOND
4 SEVEN of CLUB
Your final hand
1 FOUR of DIAMOND
2 FIVE of DIAMOND
3 FIVE of CLUB
4 SEVEN of DIAMOND
5 SEVEN of CLUB

Two pair.

1 ACE of DIAMOND
2 ACE of CLUB
3 ACE of SPADE
4 NINE of DIAMOND
5 TEN of SPADE
How many cards do you want to discard?:2
Enter card number to be removed:4
1 ACE of DIAMOND
2 ACE of CLUB
3 ACE of SPADE
4 TEN of SPADE
Enter card number to be removed:4
1 ACE of DIAMOND
2 ACE of CLUB
3 ACE of SPADE
Your final hand
1 ACE of DIAMOND
2 ACE of CLUB
3 ACE of SPADE
4 NINE of CLUB
5 TEN of HEART

Three aces.

1 FIVE of HEART
2 SIX of DIAMOND
3 NINE of DIAMOND
4 TEN of DIAMOND
5 QUEEN of DIAMOND
How many cards do you want to discard?:1
Enter card number to be removed:1
1 SIX of DIAMOND
2 NINE of DIAMOND
3 TEN of DIAMOND
4 QUEEN of DIAMOND
Your final hand
1 FIVE of DIAMOND
2 SIX of DIAMOND
3 NINE of DIAMOND
4 TEN of DIAMOND
5 QUEEN of DIAMOND

A diamond flush.

1.3 Taxman – A Game

Taxman is a game of choosing numbers, then paying a tax for the numbers you chose. The tax on a chosen number is the collection of the proper divisors of the number. The object of the game is to outscore the taxman by as much as possible.

The game begins with the player writing down a list of numbers from 1 to N. For example, the player could write down the list 1, 2, 3, 4, 5, 6, 7, 8. This list is called the original list.

The player then chooses a number from the list and the taxman takes the proper divisors of the player's chosen number. The chosen number and the proper divisors are removed from the list. For example, if the player's first choice is 8, the taxman gets 1, 2, and 4. The player's score is 8, while the taxman's score is 1+2+4, or 7. The original list is reduced to 3, 5, 6 and 7.

The player now chooses a second number. The player cannot choose 3, 5 or 7, because these numbers have no proper divisors in the reduced list. The player can choose only the 6, whereby the taxman gets the 3.

The list is reduced to 5 and 7. With no more choices available to the player, the taxman gets both the 5 and the 7, the numbers remaining in the list. The player's score is now 8 + 6, or 14, while the taxman's score increases from 7 to 7 + 5 + 7, or 19.

At each turn of the game, the player can choose any number from the list of remaining numbers, PROVIDED the number has proper divisors in the list. This provision is what provides a challenge to the game.

I will play another game and make better choices. Perhaps this will provide some insight into how to outscore the taxman. I will begin the game again with the initial list as: 1, 2, 3, 4, 5, 6, 7 and 8. My first choice is 7, and the taxman gets only the 1. The list is reduced to: 2, 3, 4, 5, 6 and 8.

My second choice is 6, and the taxman gets 2 and 3. My score is now 7 + 6, or 13, while the taxman's score is 1 + 2 + 3, or 6. The list is reduced to: 4, 5 and 8.

My third choice is 8, and the taxman gets the 4. My score is now 13 + 8, or 21 while the taxman's score is 6 + 4, or 10. The list is now reduced to 5, so with no more choices available to the player, the taxman gets the 5.

My final score is now 21, while the taxman's final score is 10 + 5, or 15.

My challenge is to write a **Python** program that enables one to play the game of **taxman**. The **Python** code can be seen below and on the next two pages.

""" The TAXMAN player enters the quantity of numbers, n. The game will consist of the player choosing numbers, first from the numbers 1 to n. The taxman receives the proper divisors of the players choice. Scores for the player and the taxman are the sum of their numbers. The taxman's numbers are removed from available choices. The game ends when the player has no choice. """

```python
def find_proper_divisors(c):
    div_lst = []
    choice = c
    for k in range(1, choice + 1):
        if choice % k == 0 and k in avail:
            div_lst.append(k)
    return div_lst

def make_a_choice():
    print (scores)
    print ('available', avail)
    choice = int(input('Choose a number from the list: '))
    divisors = find_proper_divisors(choice)
    print ('Divisors of', choice, 'are', divisors)
    if divisors[0] == sum(divisors):
        choice = 0
    return choice
```

```python
scores = {'YOU': 0, 'TAXMAN': 0}
avail = []
n = int(input('Enter the largest number in the list: '))

for j in range(1, n + 1):
    avail.append(j)
while len(avail) > 0:
    choice = make_a_choice()
    if choice != 0:
        divisors = find_proper_divisors(choice)
        avail.remove(choice)
        divisors.remove(choice)
        scores['YOU'] = scores['YOU']  + choice
        LD = len(divisors)
        while LD > 0:
            scores['TAXMAN'] = scores['TAXMAN']  + divisors[0]
            avail.remove(divisors[0])
            divisors.remove(divisors[0])
            LD = LD - 1
    else:
        LA = len(avail)
        while LA > 0 :
            scores['TAXMAN'] = scores['TAXMAN']  + avail[0]
            avail.remove(avail[0])
            LA = LA - 1
            print ('LA is', LA, avail)

print ('Final scores are')
print (scores)
```

. . .

A game played with the **Python** code is shown below.

```
>>> taxman(16)
You have 0 Taxman has 0
available [1, 2, 3, 4, 5, 6, 7, 8, 9, 10, 11, 12, 13, 14, 15, 16]
Choose a number from the list: 13

You have 13 Taxman has 1
available [2, 3, 4, 5, 6, 7, 8, 9, 10, 11, 12, 14, 15, 16]
Choose a number from the list: 14

You have 27 Taxman has 10
available [3, 4, 5, 6, 8, 9, 10, 11, 12, 15, 16]
Choose a number from the list: 9

You have 36 Taxman has 13
available [4, 5, 6, 8, 10, 11, 12, 15, 16]
Choose a number from the list: 15

You have 51 Taxman has 18
available [4, 6, 8, 10, 11, 12, 16]
Choose a number from the list: 12

You have 63 Taxman has 28
available [8, 10, 11, 16]
Choose a number from the list: 16

You have 79 Taxman has 36
available [10, 11]
Choose a number from the list: 0
Your final score is 79 Taxman scored 57
```

. . .

Chapter Two: Days, Dates and Leap Years

2.1 Zeller's Formula

There's an old poem regarding the day on which a child was born. It goes like this:

Monday's child is fair of face.
Tuesday's child is full of grace.
Wednesday's child is full of woe.
Thursday's child has far to go.
Friday's child is loving and giving.
Saturday's child works hard for his living.
And the child that is born on the Sabbath day is
bonny and blithe, and good and gay.

Perhaps you have never heard of **Zeller's Formula**. His formula will provide the day-of-the-week for any given date. The challenge is to write a **Python** program that uses **Zeller's Formula.** The program should determine the day of the week for a given date.

For a date entered as MM/DD/YYYY, **Zeller's Formula** uses the variable **M** for the month, the variable **D** for the day and the variable **Y** for the year within the century. The variable **C** for the century will come from the first YY of the date entry YYYY.

The **Python** equation for **Zeller's Formula** is expressed as:

d_n = (D + int((13 * M - 1) / 5) + C + int(C / 4) + int(Y / 4) -2 * C) % 7, where d_n is the day number in a week, Sunday is day number 1.

The variable **M** must be modified for the months January and February. For these months, add 12 to **M**. The **Python** code for the program, **Zeller** is shown below and on the next page:

```
""" Zeller's formulas for the day-of the week equals
(the day + 13 times the month minus 1 divided by 5)
plus the year Y, plus (the year divided by 4),
plus (the century divided by 4), minus twice the century,
all modulo 7. The program uses Zeller's formula to
provide the day-of-the-week for a given date.
"""

import datetime

now = datetime.datetime.now() # Need today's year from Python.
yr = int(now.year)
days = ['Sunday','Monday','Tuesday','Wednesday',
     'Thursday','Friday','Saturday']

print
('Enter the date as MM/DD/YYYY')
MM = int(input('Enter the month: '))
DD = int(input('Enter the day: '))
YYYY = int(input('Enter the year: '))
date = [MM,DD,YYYY]
```

```
D = date[1]
Y = date[2] % 100
C = int(date[2] / 100)
M = date[0] - 2
if M < 1:       # Month number must be adjusted.
    M = M + 12
    Y = Y - 1


# day_num is Zeller's formula.
day_num = (D + int((13 * M - 1) / 5) + Y + int(Y / 4) + int(C / 4) - 2 * C) % 7


if YYYY < yr:
    print ('The date', date[0], '/', D, '/', date[2])
    print ('was on a', days[day_num])
else:
    print ('The date', date[0], '/', D, '/', date[2])
    print ('will be on a', days[day_num])
```
· · ·

Abraham Lincoln, the 16th president of the United States of America, was assassinated on April 15th, 1865.
Enter the date as MM/DD/YYYY
Enter the month: 4
Enter the day: 15
Enter the year: 1865
The date 4 / 15 / 1865
was on a Saturday

The day known as 9/11, was the day
the USA was attacked by terrorist.
Enter the date as MM/DD/YYYY
Enter the month: 9
Enter the day: 11
Enter the year: 2001
The date 9 / 11 / 2001
was on a Tuesday

Let's check on Christmas for the year 2024.
Enter the date as MM/DD/YYYY
Enter the month: 12
Enter the day: 25
Enter the year: 2024
The date 12 / 25 / 2024
will be on a Wednesday

On July 22, 2028, Australia and New Zealand will
witness a total solar eclipse.
Enter the date as MM/DD/YYYY
Enter the month: 7
Enter the day: 22
Enter the year: 2028
The date 7 / 22 / 2028
will be on a Saturday

. . .

2.2 Leap Years

The challenge is to write a **Python** program that calculates and displays a list of the leap years between two given dates. The list must be inclusive of the two dates. The solution will support the problem solved in the next section.

To determine if a year, Y, is a leap year, one first determines if 4 divides Y evenly. If 4 divides Y evenly, then Y is a multiple of 4. I prefer the phrase '*Y is a multiple of 4*' to the phrase '*4 divides Y evenly.*' If Y is not a multiple of 4, then Y is not a leap year. For example, 2016 was a leap year, while 2017 was not a leap year.

Continuing, if Y is a multiple of 4, one must next determine if Y is a multiple of 100. If so, one must also determine if Y is a multiple of 400.

If Y is a multiple of both 100 and 400, Y is a leap year. Otherwise Y is not a leap year. For example, 2200 is a leap year, while 2300 is not a leap year.

The **Python** program to solve this problem will first request the two years in the format YYYY, i.e., a four-digit number. See the code of the program on the next page.

+

""" The program, leap_years_between, will
display the **leap years** between two given years.
"""

```
def is_a_leap_year(y):
    if y % 4 == 0:
        return True
    if y % 100 == 100 and y % 400 > 0:
        return false

# Main program:

leap_years = []
years = []
y1 = int(input('Enter a year: '))
y2 = int(input('Enter a year: '))
if y1 > y2:
    temp = y1         # Need for first year to be
    y1 = y2           # earlier than second year.
    y2 = temp

for j in range(y1, y2 + 1):
    years.append(j)
years.sort()

for a_year in years:
    leap = is_a_leap_year(a_year)
    if leap:
        leap_years.append(a_year)

print ('Leap years from', y1, 'to', y2)
print (leap_years)
```

. . .

A result of executing the program is shown below:

>>> Leap_years_between()
Enter a year:1999
Enter a year:2010
Leap years from 1999 to 2010
[2000, 2004, 2008]

2.3 Number of Days Between Two Dates

The challenge is to write a **Python** program to calculate and display the number of days between two given dates. By between, I mean inclusive of the two dates.

I have a paper-and-pencil process to count the number of days from one date to a future date. My process uses the formula $M - N + 1$ for the quantity of numbers from N to M. For example, the quantity of numbers from 1 to 3 is $(3 - 1 + 1)$, or 3, while the quantity of numbers from 10 to 20 is $20 - 10 + 1$, or 11.

I also need to have a list of the number of days in each month of a non-leap year. The list is 31, 28, 31, 30, 31, 30, 31, 31, 30, 31, 30, 31. I will use the leap-year program from Section 2.2 for a more accurate count.

To calculate the number of days from March 4, 2001, and September 23, 2005, inclusive, I first count the number of days from March 4 to March 31. The number of days in March is $(31 - 4 + 1)$, or 28.

I next count the number of days in April through December of 2001. This count is
$30 + 31 + 30 + 31 + 31 + 30 + 31 + 30 + 31$, or 275.

Secondly, I count the number of days in the years 2002, 2003 and 2004. This count is 3 * 365, or 1095.

Next, I count the days from January to August. This count is $31 + 28 + 31 + 30 + 31 + 30 + 31 + 31$, or 243.

Finally, I count the days in September, i.e., the number of days from September 1 to September 23, inclusively. This count is 23.

We now have the total number of days from March 4, 2001 to September 23, 2005 as $28 + 275 + 1095 + 243 + 23$, or 1,664. From Section 2.2, we found 2004 was a leap year, so we must add one more day. The total number of days is $1,664 + 1$, or 1,665.

In general, given two dates, M1/D1/Y1 and M2/D2/Y2, we need the number of years exclusive of Y1 and Y2. This number will be $[(Y2 - 1) - (Y1 + 1) + 1]$, or $\boldsymbol{Y2 - Y1 - 1}$. This formula is an application of the formula $M - N + 1$: a formula for the quantity of numbers from N to M.

Using the example above - March 4, 2001 to September 23, 2005 – the number of years from 2001 to 2005 equals, or $2005 - 2001 - 1$, or 3.

. . .

I shall simplify the coding by making two assumptions. Specifically, I shall assume that the two given dates are valid, and that the second date is later than the first. The code for the **Python** program is shown below and on the next page.

""" The program, Number_of_days_between_two_dates, calculates the **number of days between** to given dates.
"""

```python
def get_a_date():
    print ('Enter the date as MM/DD/YYYY')
    MM = int(input('Enter the month: '))
    DD = int(input('Enter the day: '))
    YYYY = int(input('Enter the year: '))
    date = [MM, DD, YYYY]
    return date

# Main program:

# Days is a list of the numbers of days in each non-leap year month.
days=[31, 28, 31, 30, 31, 30, 31, 31, 30, 31, 30, 31]

date1 = get_a_date()
m1 = date1[0]
d1 = date1[1]
y1 = date1[2]
n1 = days[m1 - 1] - d1 + 1 # number of days in the first
                           # month of the first year.
```

```python
n2 = 0
for j in range(m1, 12):
    n2 = n2 + days[j]   # number of days in the reminder
                        # of the months of the first year

date2 = get_a_date()
m2 = date2[0]
d2 = date2[1]
y2 = date2[2]

n3 = 365 * max(y2 - y1 - 1, 0)
# n3 is the number days in the months
# between the first month and the
# first day of the last year.

n4 = 0
for j in range(0, m2 - 1):
    n4 = n4 + days[j]
# n4 is the number of days in the last year.

n5 = n1 + n2 + n3 + n4 + d2

print ('Number of days from', date1, 'to', date2, 'inclusive, is', n5)
```
. . .

An execution of the program is shown below:

```
>>> count_days()
Enter the date as MM/DD/YYYY
Enter the month: 3
Enter the day: 4
Enter the year: 2001
Enter the date as MM/DD/YYYY
Enter the month: 9
Enter the day: 23
Enter the year: 2005
28 275 243 1095 23
Number of days from [3, 4, 2001] to [9, 23, 2005],
inclusive, is 1664
```

Because 2004 was a leap year, the number of days from March 4, 2001 to September 23, 2005 is $1,664 + 1$, or 1,665.

. . .

Chapter Three: Some Special Numbers

3.1 Least Common Multiple and the Greatest Common Divisor

Students often find adding fractions to be quite challenging. For example, to add $\frac{5}{14}$ and $\frac{2}{21}$ one must determine a common denominator for the two fractions. Teachers usually require students to determine the least common denominator. The least common denominator is the smallest number which is a multiple of both denominators, so it is also called the least common multiple and is abbreviated as the LCM.

To determine the LCM of $\frac{5}{14}$ and $\frac{2}{21}$, students will express 14 as 2 * 7 and express 21 as 3 * 7, then reason that the LCM is 2 * 3 * 7 or 42. They then express the two fractions as $\frac{5*3}{42}$ and $\frac{2*5}{42}$, or $\frac{15}{42}$ and $\frac{10}{42}$ for the answer $\frac{25}{42}$.

In Chapter Five, we will visit Euclid's Algorithm, a numerical process he created to determine the greatest common divisor, or GCD of two numbers. For example, 7 divides both 21 (21 = 3 * 7) and 14 (14 = 2 * 7) and 7 is the largest number that will divide both 21 and 14.

By expressing 14 as 2 * 7 and expressing 21 as 3 * 7, the product 14 * 21 can be expressed as 2 * 7 * 3 * 7. The GCD of 14 and 21 is 7. So, 14 * 21 equals the GCD times the LCM. In general, the product of N and M equals the product of their GCD and LCM. We have the formulas:

$$N * M = GCD * LCM \text{ and } LCM = \frac{N * M}{GCD}.$$

I will use the formula $LCM = \frac{N * M}{GCD}$ in a **Python** program to determine the LCM of two denominators.

My challenge is to write a **Python** program that will determine both the GCD and LCM of two given numbers.

A description of the process to find the GCD of N and M follows:

Given two numbers N and M, the program creates three lists: N-list consisting of all proper divisors of N except 1, M-list consisting of all proper divisors of M except 1 and NM-list consisting of all divisors of both N and M.

Next, create the list nm-list consisting of the unduplicated products, p * q, where p and q are from the NM-list, and p * q divides both N and M. The largest product in the nm-list is the GCD of N and M.

For example, given $N = 48$ and $M = 36$, the N-list will be [2, 3, 4, 6, 8, 12, 16, 24], while the M-list will be [2, 3, 4, 6, 9, 12, 18]. Therefore, the NM-list will be [2, 3, 4, 6, 12], then the nm-list will be [2 * 2, 2 * 3, 2 * 6], or [4, 6, 12].

The maximum of [4, 6, 12] is 12, so 12 is the GCD of 48 and 36.

The code for the program is shown below and on the next page.

```
""" Program finds the GCD (greatest common divisor)
and the LCM (least common multiple) of n and m.
"""


# div_lst will be a list of the proper divisors of n.
def find_divisors(n):
    div_lst=[]
    for k in range(2, n - 1):
        if n % k == 0:
            div_lst.append(k)
    return div_lst
```

```python
def GCD(n, m):
    N = []
    M = []
    NM = []
    nm = []
    N = find_divisors(n)
    nm = []
    M = find_divisors(m)
    if len(N) * len(M) != 0:
        for j in range(len(N)):
            c = N[j]
            if c in M:
                NM.append(c)

        for j in range(len(NM)):
            for k in range(j, len(NM)):
                p = NM[j]
                q = NM[k]
                r = NM[j] * NM[k]
                if n % r == 0 and m % r == 0 and r not in nm:
                    nm.append(r)
                if p == q:
                    nm.append(p)
    return nm
```

```python
# Main program:
nm = []
n = int(input('Enter a number: '))
m = int(input('Enter a larger number: '))
print('')
nm = GCD(n, m)
if nm == []:
    GCD = 1
else:
    GCD = max(nm)
print('Greatest common divisor of', n, 'and', m, 'is', GCD)
print('')
LCM = int((n * m) / GCD)
print('Least common multiple of', n, 'and', m, 'is', LCM)
```

. . .

Several executions of the program are shown below and on the next page.

Enter a number: 36
Enter a larger number: 48

Greatest common divisor of 36 and 48 is 12

Least common multiple of 36 and 48 is 144

Enter a number: 90
Enter a larger number: 100

Greatest common divisor of 90 and 100 is 10

Least common multiple of 90 and 100 is 900

Enter a number: 100
Enter a larger number: 135

Greatest common divisor of 100 and 135 is 5

Least common multiple of 100 and 135 is 2700

Enter a number: 255
Enter a larger number: 3927

Greatest common divisor of 255 and 3927 is 51

Least common multiple of 255 and 3927 is 19635

. . .

3.2 Perfect Numbers

Pythagoras lived sometime between 580 and 500 BCE. Legend has it that Pythagoras believed that numbers held mystical and religious powers. He reportedly formed a group of followers, the Pythagoreans, who believed about numbers as he did. This cult believed that numbers were godly and deserved respect. For example, 2 is the smallest female number and 3 the smallest male number, so 5, the sum of 2 and 3 stood for marriage. The moon, sun, and the planets formed seven heavenly objects, so the number 7 was awesome.

The Pythagoreans believed some numbers were **perfect.** For example, God took six days to create the universe, so the number 6 is a perfect number. The number of days between one full moon and the next is 28, so the number 28 is a perfect number.

The numbers 6 and 28 both have the property of being equal to the sum of their proper divisors. The numbers 1, 2, and 3 are the proper divisors of 6, while $6 = 1 + 2 + 3$. The numbers 1, 2, 4, 7 and 14 are the proper divisors of 28, while $28 = 1 + 2 + 4 + 7 + 14$.

The Pythagoreans defined a number to be **perfect** if it is equal to the sum of its proper divisors.

Euclid lived 300 years after the time of Pythagoras. He, too, was interested in **perfect numbers** and proved an important theorem regarding these numbers. I shall refer to this theorem as Euclid's **Perfect-Prime Theorem** and discuss it later in Chapter Four.

Euclid knew of only the first four perfect numbers: 6, 28, 496 and 8,128; yet his **Perfect-Prime Theorem promised** there are more. The next perfect number, 33,550,336, was found long after Euclid's time.

The challenge is to write a **Python** program to determine if a number is a **perfect number**, i.e., equal to the sum of its proper divisors.

A number N divides another number M if dividing M by N leaves a zero remainder. For example: dividing 39 by 3 equals 13 with no remainder, because $39 = 3 * 13$. We can therefore say 39 is both a multiple of 3 and a multiple of 13.

The **Python** operator % provides remainders. For example, $39 \% 4 = 3$, because $39 = 4 * 9 + 3$. While $39 \% 3 = 0$, because $39 = 3 * 13 + 0$.

The **Python** code for the program is shown on the next page.

```python
""" Program will determine if n is a perfect number.
"""

n = int(input('Enter a number: '))
proper_divisors = [1]

for j in range(2, n):
    if n % j == 0:
        proper_divisors.append(j)

print ('proper_divisors of', n, 'are')
print (proper_divisors)

SUM = sum(proper_divisors)
if SUM == n:
    print (n,'is a perfect number')
else:
    print (n,'is not a perfect number')
```

. . .

Several executions of the program are shown below:

Enter a number: 496
proper_divisors of 496 are
[1, 2, 4, 8, 16, 31, 62, 124, 248]
496 is a perfect number

Enter a number: 8128
proper_divisors of 8128 are
[1, 2, 4, 8, 16, 32, 64, 127, 254, 508, 1016, 2032, 4064]
8128 is a perfect number

Enter a number: 1000
proper_divisors of 1000 are
[1, 2, 4, 5, 8, 10, 20, 25, 40, 50, 100, 125, 200, 250, 500]
1000 is not a perfect number

Enter a number: 33550336
proper_divisors of 33550336 are
[1, 2, 4, 8, 16, 32, 64, 128, 256, 512, 1024, 2048, 4096,
8191, 16382, 32764, 65528, 131056, 262112, 524224,
1048448, 2096896, 4193792, 8387584, 16775168]
33550336 is a perfect number

. . .

3.3 Powers-of-2

We next explore powers of the number 2, such as 2, 4, 8, 16 and 32. These five powers of 2 can be expressed as $2^1, 2^2, 2^3, 2^4$ and 2^5. The number 1 is also a power of 2, specifically, $1 = 2^0$.

The following list of powers of 2 will help with some calculations:

$2^0 = 1.$ $2^1 = 2.$ $2^2 = 4.$ $2^3 = 8.$ $2^4 = 16.$ $2^5 = 32.$

$2^6 = 64.$ $2^7 = 128.$ $2^8 = 256.$ $2^9 = 512.$

The following equations will reveal an important formula.

$2^0 + 2^1 = 3 = (2^2 - 1).$
$2^0 + 2^1 + 2^2 = 7 = (2^3 - 1).$
$2^0 + 2^1 + 2^2 + 2^3 = 15 = (2^4 - 1).$
$2^0 + 2^1 + 2^2 + 2^3 + 2^4 = 31 = (2^5 - 1).$
$2^0 + 2^1 + 2^2 + 2^3 + 2^4 + 2^5 = 63 = (2^6 - 1).$
$2^0 + 2^1 + 2^2 + 2^3 + 2^4 + 2^5 + 2^6 = 127 = (2^7 - 1).$

From observation, we have the formula:

$$2^0 + 2^1 + 2^2 + 2^3 + \cdots + 2^N = 2^{N+1} - 1.$$

$\cdots$

In Section 3.1, I mentioned Euclid's **Perfect-Prime Theorem** regarding perfect numbers. This theorem involves powers of 2, one reason that powers of 2 have mathematical importance. Powers of 2 are highly related to the **digital technology/binary technology** used in calculators, computers, cars and many common household appliances.

When writing, authors might refer to pairs and couples with the word 'two', or the word 'Two' or with the symbol '2'. When they refer to counting, they may be writing about adding 2. Each of these references, the letter 'T' in the word 'Two', the letter 't' in the word 'two', the symbol '2' and the notion of adding 2 are represented differently in a computer.

Digital technology represents characters and symbols using a sequence of 8 bits, where each eight-bit sequence equals **a sum of powers of 2**.

A bit is either a zero or a one (i.e., a 0 or a 1.) The symbol '2' is represented by the eight-bit sequence 00110010. This eight-bit binary number equals the sum $2^1 + 2^4 + 2^5$ (i.e., a **sum of powers of 2**.)

The capitol letter 'T' in the word 'Two' is represented by the eight-bit sequence 01010100. This eight-bit binary number equals the sum, $2^2 + 2^4 + 2^6$.

The letter 't' in the word 'two' is represented by the eight-bit sequence 01110100. This eight-bit binary number equals the sum, $2^2 + 2^4 + 2^5 + 2^6$.

When the computer adds the number 2 and the number 3, it uses the binary number 00000010 for 2 and the binary number 00000011 for 3. The answer is 00000101 which is the binary number for 5. The symbol 5 is represented as 00110101. This eight-bit binary number is equals the sum, $2^0 + 2^2 + 2^4 + 2^5$.

Below, I show how to count in binary.

Counting from 1 to 9 using eight-bit binary numbers, we have:
1 = 00000001
2 = 00000010
3 = 00000011
4 = 00000100
5 = 00000101
6 = 00000110
7 = 00000111
8 = 00001000
9 = 00001001

Notice that when adding 1 in base-2 arithmetic acts like adding 9 in base-10 (e.g., in base-2, 1 + 1 = 10, and 11 + 1 = 100, whereas in base-10, 1 + 9 = 10, and 21 + 9 = 30).

My challenge is to write a **Python** program that converts a base-10 number to an eight-bit binary number. The code for the program is shown below:

```python
""" Program converts a base-10 number that is less than 128 to its
binary form.
"""

n = int(input('Enter a number to convert to binary: '))

index_list = [6, 5, 4, 3, 2, 1, 0]
        # List of each power of 2's
        # positions in a binary number.
        # e.g., position of 8, 2^3 is 3.
        # binry will be the list of bits
binry = [0]
if n < 128:
    m = n
    for power in index_list:
        if m - 2**power >= 0:
            binry.append(1)
        else:
            binry.append(0)
        if m - 2**power >=0:
            m = m - 2**power
    print(n, 'converted to binary is', binry)
```

```
else:
    print(n, 'is too large to convert.')
```

. . .

Several executions are shown below:

Enter a number to convert to binary: 65
65 converted to binary is [0, 1, 0, 0, 0, 0, 0, 1]

Enter a number to convert to binary: 100
100 converted to binary is [0, 1, 1, 0, 0, 1, 0, 0]

Enter a number to convert to binary: 127
127 converted to binary is [0, 1, 1, 1, 1, 1, 1, 1]

Enter a number to convert to binary: 200
200 is too large to convert.

. . .

For displaying and printing letters and characters, the computer uses the ASCII codes adopted in 1967 by the electronics industry. My next challenge is to write a **Python** program that first produces the ASCII for a character then converts the ASCII code number to binary.

In **Python**, a single character is considered to be a **string**. To produce the ASCII code for a character, I use **Python**'s 'ord' function. The 'ord' function returns the ASCII number for a character. For example ord('=') returns the number 61.

To convert the ASCII code number to binary, I will use the code of the program **convert_n_to_binary** as a function.

The program will enable the user to display a group of consecutive characters. For each character, the program will display the character, its ASCII code and the binary form of ASCII code number. The **Python** code for the program is shown the next page.

""" For the program ASCII_and_Binary, the user enters a keyboard character as the first character in the list consecutive characters. The use then enters the length of the list of consecutive characters. The program creates the list of characters and displays each character along with its ASCII code and the binary form of its ASCII code.
"""

```python
# Convert a base-10 number to binary
def convert_to_binary(n):
    index_list = [6, 5, 4, 3, 2, 1, 0]
                # List of each power of 2's
                # positions in a binary number.
                # e.g., position of 8, 2^3 is 3.

# bin will be the list of bits
    bin = [0]
    m = n
    for power in index_list:
        if m - 2**power >= 0:
            bin.append(1)
        else:
            bin.append(0)

        if m - 2**power >= 0:
            m = m - 2**power
    return bin
```

Main program:

```python
ch = input('Enter the first character in the list: ')
characters = [ch]
length = int(input('Enter the length of the list: '))
first_character = ord(ch)
last_character = first_character + length
for j in range(1, length):
    char = chr(first_character + j)
    characters.append(char)

for char in characters:
    n = ord(char)
    binry = convert_to_binary(n)
    print (char, 'has ASCII code', n,'and binary form', binry)
```

. . .

Executions of the program are shown on the next two pages.

Enter the first character in the list: A
Enter the length of the list: 26
A has ASCII code 65 and binary form [0, 1, 0, 0, 0, 0, 0, 1]
B has ASCII code 66 and binary form [0, 1, 0, 0, 0, 0, 1, 0]
C has ASCII code 67 and binary form [0, 1, 0, 0, 0, 0, 1, 1]
D has ASCII code 68 and binary form [0, 1, 0, 0, 0, 1, 0, 0]
E has ASCII code 69 and binary form [0, 1, 0, 0, 0, 1, 0, 1]
F has ASCII code 70 and binary form [0, 1, 0, 0, 0, 1, 1, 0]
G has ASCII code 71 and binary form [0, 1, 0, 0, 0, 1, 1, 1]
H has ASCII code 72 and binary form [0, 1, 0, 0, 1, 0, 0, 0]
I has ASCII code 73 and binary form [0, 1, 0, 0, 1, 0, 0, 1]
J has ASCII code 74 and binary form [0, 1, 0, 0, 1, 0, 1, 0]
K has ASCII code 75 and binary form [0, 1, 0, 0, 1, 0, 1, 1]
L has ASCII code 76 and binary form [0, 1, 0, 0, 1, 1, 0, 0]
M has ASCII code 77 and binary form [0, 1, 0, 0, 1, 1, 0, 1]
N has ASCII code 78 and binary form [0, 1, 0, 0, 1, 1, 1, 0]
O has ASCII code 79 and binary form [0, 1, 0, 0, 1, 1, 1, 1]
P has ASCII code 80 and binary form [0, 1, 0, 1, 0, 0, 0, 0]
Q has ASCII code 81 and binary form [0, 1, 0, 1, 0, 0, 0, 1]
R has ASCII code 82 and binary form [0, 1, 0, 1, 0, 0, 1, 0]
S has ASCII code 83 and binary form [0, 1, 0, 1, 0, 0, 1, 1]
T has ASCII code 84 and binary form [0, 1, 0, 1, 0, 1, 0, 0]
U has ASCII code 85 and binary form [0, 1, 0, 1, 0, 1, 0, 1]
V has ASCII code 86 and binary form [0, 1, 0, 1, 0, 1, 1, 0]
W has ASCII code 87 and binary form [0, 1, 0, 1, 0, 1, 1, 1]
X has ASCII code 88 and binary form [0, 1, 0, 1, 1, 0, 0, 0]
Y has ASCII code 89 and binary form [0, 1, 0, 1, 1, 0, 0, 1]
Z has ASCII code 90 and binary form [0, 1, 0, 1, 1, 0, 1, 0]

Enter the first character in the list: a
Enter the length of the list: 26
a has ASCII code 97 and binary form [0, 1, 1, 0, 0, 0, 0, 1]
b has ASCII code 98 and binary form [0, 1, 1, 0, 0, 0, 1, 0]
c has ASCII code 99 and binary form [0, 1, 1, 0, 0, 0, 1, 1]
d has ASCII code 100 and binary form [0, 1, 1, 0, 0, 1, 0, 0]
e has ASCII code 101 and binary form [0, 1, 1, 0, 0, 1, 0, 1]
f has ASCII code 102 and binary form [0, 1, 1, 0, 0, 1, 1, 0]
g has ASCII code 103 and binary form [0, 1, 1, 0, 0, 1, 1, 1]
h has ASCII code 104 and binary form [0, 1, 1, 0, 1, 0, 0, 0]
i has ASCII code 105 and binary form [0, 1, 1, 0, 1, 0, 0, 1]
j has ASCII code 106 and binary form [0, 1, 1, 0, 1, 0, 1, 0]
k has ASCII code 107 and binary form [0, 1, 1, 0, 1, 0, 1, 1]
l has ASCII code 108 and binary form [0, 1, 1, 0, 1, 1, 0, 0]
m has ASCII code 109 and binary form [0, 1, 1, 0, 1, 1, 0, 1]
n has ASCII code 110 and binary form [0, 1, 1, 0, 1, 1, 1, 0]
o has ASCII code 111 and binary form [0, 1, 1, 0, 1, 1, 1, 1]
p has ASCII code 112 and binary form [0, 1, 1, 1, 0, 0, 0, 0]
q has ASCII code 113 and binary form [0, 1, 1, 1, 0, 0, 0, 1]
r has ASCII code 114 and binary form [0, 1, 1, 1, 0, 0, 1, 0]
s has ASCII code 115 and binary form [0, 1, 1, 1, 0, 0, 1, 1]
t has ASCII code 116 and binary form [0, 1, 1, 1, 0, 1, 0, 0]
u has ASCII code 117 and binary form [0, 1, 1, 1, 0, 1, 0, 1]
v has ASCII code 118 and binary form [0, 1, 1, 1, 0, 1, 1, 0]
w has ASCII code 119 and binary form [0, 1, 1, 1, 0, 1, 1, 1]
x has ASCII code 120 and binary form [0, 1, 1, 1, 1, 0, 0, 0]
y has ASCII code 121 and binary form [0, 1, 1, 1, 1, 0, 0, 1]
z has ASCII code 122 and binary form [0, 1, 1, 1, 1, 0, 1, 0]

. . .

Enter the first character in the list: 0
Enter the length of the list: 10
0 has ASCII code 48 and binary form [0, 0, 1, 1, 0, 0, 0, 0]
1 has ASCII code 49 and binary form [0, 0, 1, 1, 0, 0, 0, 1]
2 has ASCII code 50 and binary form [0, 0, 1, 1, 0, 0, 1, 0]
3 has ASCII code 51 and binary form [0, 0, 1, 1, 0, 0, 1, 1]
4 has ASCII code 52 and binary form [0, 0, 1, 1, 0, 1, 0, 0]
5 has ASCII code 53 and binary form [0, 0, 1, 1, 0, 1, 0, 1]
6 has ASCII code 54 and binary form [0, 0, 1, 1, 0, 1, 1, 0]
7 has ASCII code 55 and binary form [0, 0, 1, 1, 0, 1, 1, 1]
8 has ASCII code 56 and binary form [0, 0, 1, 1, 1, 0, 0, 0]
9 has ASCII code 57 and binary form [0, 0, 1, 1, 1, 0, 0, 1]

3.4 Pythagorean Triples

When designing a house, an architect must keep walls **perpendicular** to floors. Corners of doorways and windows usually need to form **right angles**. As ancients designed and constructed their dwellings, they made measurements and discovered the sides forming right angles are related to certain kinds of numbers.

An angle formed by two perpendicular sides will have a third side joining these two to form a **right triangle**. This third non-perpendicular side is longer than the other two sides. It's called the **hypotenuse** of the right triangle.

For perpendicular sides measuring 3 units and 4 units, ancient builders found the hypotenuse measured 5 units. For perpendicular sides measuring 5 units and 12 units, they found the hypotenuse measured 13 units.

Number-triples like as 3-4-5 and 5-12-13, relating to right angles, led the Pythagoreans to **perfect squares:** numbers that are the squares of numbers.

For the triple 3-4-5, we have $3^2 + 4^2 = 5^2$.

For the triple 5-12-13, we have $5^2 + 12^2 = 13^2$.

The first ten perfect squares are 1, 4, 9, 16, 25, 36, 49, 64, 81 and 100. To square a number is to multiply it times itself. When squaring the number 3, we use the notations 3 * 3 or 3^2.

Numbers A, B and C, with the property $A^2 + B^2 = C^2$, are called **Pythagorean Triples** and are written as the triple A-B-C.

The Pythagoreans probably discovered several triples, measurements forming right angles. They proved:

*Two sides will be perpendicular when the sum of the squares of the sides is a **perfect square**.*

An angle formed by sides A and B will form a right angle when $A^2 + B^2$ **is a perfect square**. Their discovery is known as the **Pythagorean Theorem.**

Euclid is given credit for finding a formulation to generate all Pythagorean Triples. To generate a triple, substitute two whole numbers M and N, where M > N, into the three formulas:

$A = M^2 - N^2,$ $B = 2MN,$ $C = M^2 + N^2.$

For example, with M = 2 and N = 3, then
$A = 9 - 4 = 5, B = 2 * 2 * 3 = 12$ and
$C = 9 + 4 = 13$, where $5^2 + 12^2 = 13^2$.

Also, with M = 1 and N = 5, we have
A = 25 – 1 = 24, B = 2 * 1 * 5 = 10, and C = 25 + 1 = 26, where $24^2 + 10^2 = 26^2$. Note that the triple 10-24-26 is a multiple of the triple 5-12-13, so 10-24-16 is not a **primitive triple**. The program should generate only **primitive triples**.

The challenge is to write a **Python** program using **Euclid's formulation** to generate and display a list of Pythagorean Triples. The process should be extendable to potentially all Pythagorean Triples. The process will use an ordering of the pairs (N, M), where M is not equal to N. The following is an ordered list of 21 ordered pairs:
(1, 2),
(1, 3), (2, 3),
(1, 4), (2, 4), (3, 4),
(1, 5), (2, 5), (3, 5), (4, 5),
(1, 6), (2, 6), (3, 6), (4, 6), (5, 6),
(1, 7), (2, 7), (3, 7), (4, 7), (5, 7), (6, 7),
etc.

The configuration of the list was chosen to convince the reader that an extension of the list will potentially contain every possible ordered pair (N, M), where N < M.

The **Python** program will generate a similar list beginning with (1, 2), then use the pairs and Euclid's three formulas, $A = M^2 - N^2$, $B = 2MN$ and $C = M^2 + N^2$ to calculate the associated Pythagorean Triples. If A and B have a common divisor, then the triple A-B-C will not be included.

The **Python** code for the program is shown below and on the next two pages.

""" The program, pythag_triples, creates a list of ordered pairs of numbers [n, m] and uses the pairs along with Euclid's formulation to create a list of primitive Pythagorean Triples.
"""

```python
# div_lst will be a list of the proper divisors of n.
def find_divisors(n):
    div_lst = []
    for k in range(2, n + 1):
        if n % k == 0:
            div_lst.append(k)
    return div_lst

def primitive(n, m):
        T = True
        a = m**2-n**2       # If A = m^2 - n^2 and B = 2nm have
        b = 2*n*m           # a common factor, then A – B - C
        small = min(a, b)    # is not a primitive triple.
        large = max(a, b)
        s_lst = find_divisors(small)
        l_lst = find_divisors(large)
        for j in s_lst:
            if j in l_lst:
                T = False
                break
        return T
```

```python
print ('Enter the last coordinate of the pairs [n, m]')
n = int(input('used to generate the Pythagorean Triples: '))
n = n + 1
triples = []              # list of Pythagorean Triples
pairs = []                # list of ordered pairs of numbers
prm_pairs = []

for j in range(1, n + 1):      # Create a list of ordered pairs
    for k in range(j + 1, n):  # (1, 2), (1, 3), ...,(1, n - 1)
        p = [j, k]             # (2,3), (2,4), ...,(2, n - 1)
        pairs.append(p)        # (3, 4), (3, 5), ..., (3, n - 1), etc.

for j in range(len(pairs)):
    p = pairs[j]
    f0 = p[0]
    f1 = p[1]
    a = f1**2 - f0**2     # Use Euclid's three formulas.
    b = 2 * f0 * f1
    if primitive(f0, f1):
        prm_pairs.append(p)
        c = f0**2 + f1**2
        t = [a, b, c]
        triples.append(t)
print ('')
print ('The', len(prm_pairs), 'pairs')
print (prm_pairs)
print ('')
print ('generate the', len(prm_pairs), 'primitive Pythagorean Triples.')
print (triples)
```

. . .

An execution of the program is shown below:

Enter the last coordinate of the pairs [n, m]
used to generate the Pythagorean Triples: 8

The 15 pairs
[[1, 2], [1, 4], [1, 6], [1, 8],
[2, 3], [2, 5], [2, 7], [3, 4],
[3, 8], [4, 5], [4, 7], [5, 6],
[5, 8], [6, 7], [7, 8]]

generate the 15 primitive Pythagorean Triples.
[[3, 4, 5], [15, 8, 17], [35, 12, 37], [63, 16, 65],
[5, 12, 13], [21, 20, 29], [45, 28, 53], [7, 24, 25],
[55, 48, 73], [9, 40, 41], [33, 56, 65], [11, 60, 61],
[39, 80, 89], [13, 84, 85], [15, 112, 113]]

For example, the ninth pair [3, 8] generated the ninth
triple, 55 – 48 - 73.

. . .

The three formulas, $A = M^2 - N^2$, $B = 2MN$ and $C = M^2 + N^2$, provide an **unlimited quantity** of Pythagorean Triples. The collection of Pythagorean Triples is infinite.

$\cdots$

Euclid's formulation process is **reversible** (i.e., given a Pythagorean Triple, it is possible to find the M and N that generate the triple). For example, given the triple $12 - 35 - 37$, we have $A = 35 = M^2 - N^2$, $B = 12 = 2MN$ and $C = 37 = M^2 + N^2$.

Adding A and C, we have $2M^2 = 35 + 37$, so $M^2 = 36$, and M = 6. From $12 = 2 * 6 * N$, we have $N = 1$. We conclude that the pair $[1, 6]$ will generate 12-35-37.

From the example, we can formulate the reversing process. Given A-B-C as a Pythagorean Triple, we have M equal to the square root of A plus C divided by 2, or

$$M = \sqrt{\frac{A+C}{2}}.$$

From $B = 2MN$, we also have N equal to B divided by twice M, or $N = \dfrac{B}{2M}$.

My challenge it to write a **Python** program to perform this **reversing process** on a given Pythagorean Triple. The program must first verify that the given triple A-B-C is, in fact, a Pythagorean Triple. This means determining if $A^2 + B^2$ equals C^2.

The program must also verify that both M and N are whole numbers. For
 this purpose, the program will use the 'int' function, or the **integer-value** function. The **integer-value** of a decimal number is the leading whole number of the decimal number. For example, $\sqrt{170}$ is **approximately** equal to 13.03840, so the **integer-value** of $\sqrt{170}$ equals 13.

Finally, the program must verify that the pair [N, M] generates the given triple A-B-C. The program will use Euclid's formulas for this verification. The code for the program is shown on the next two pages.

. . .

""" The program, reverse.py, finds the pair (N, M) that generates a given Pythagorean Triple.
"""

```python
def get_a_triple():
    t = []
    print('Enter a triple as A, B, and C')
    a = int(input('A is '))
    t.append(a)
    b = int(input('B is '))
    t.append(b)
    c = int(input('C is '))
    t.append(c)
    return t

def its_a_triple(t):
    a = t[0]
    b = t[1]
    c = t[2]
    As = a**2 + b**2
    Cs = c**2
    if As != Cs:
        return False
    else:
        return True
```

```python
# Main program:
trip = get_a_triple()
a = trip[0]
b = trip[1]
c = trip[2]

if its_a_triple(trip):
    m = ((a + c) / 2)**0.5
    n = b / (2 * m)
    M = int(m)
    N = int(n)
    A = M**2 - N**2        # Apply Euclid's formulas.
    B = 2 * N * M
    C = M**2 + N**2
    print ('The pair [', N, ',', M, '] generates the triple', A, '-',
B, '-', C)
else:
    print (a, '-', b, '-', c, 'not a Pythagorean-Triple')
                            . . .
```

Several executions of the program are shown below:

Enter a triple as A, B, and C
A is 35
B is 12
C is 37
The integer-value of 6.0 is 6
The integer-value of 1.0 is 1
The pair [1 , 6] generates the triple 35 - 12 - 37

Enter a triple as A, B, and C
A is 33
B is 56
C is 65
The integer-value of 7.0 is 7
The integer-value of 4.0 is 4
The pair [4 , 7] generates the triple 33 - 56 - 65

Enter a triple as A, B, and C
A is 391
B is 120
C is 409
The integer-value of 20.0 is 20
The integer-value of 3.0 is 3
The pair [3 , 20] generates the triple 391 - 120 - 409

· · ·

Chapter Four: Introduction to Prime Numbers

4.1 A First Exploration of Prime Numbers

The collection of **prime numbers** is the most important set of whole numbers in all of mathematics. These numbers have been studied by mathematicians since the time of the Pythagoreans. Every number except 1 can be expressed in terms of **prime number.**

A number is a **prime number** if it has no proper divisors other than 1. A more formal definition follows: a number P is a **prime number** if P has **exactly two divisors**, the number 1 and the number P itself.

This formal definition eliminates the number 1 as a prime number because it has only one divisor, itself. To simplify statements regarding prime numbers, mathematicians preferred to exclude 1 as a prime number.

The first seven prime numbers are 2, 3, 5, 7, 11, 13, and 17. Every non-prime number except the number 1 is a multiple of at least one prime number. Below are some examples:

126 = 2*3*3*7.   300 =2*2*3*5*5.

3,185 = 5*7*7*13.   28,611=3*3*11*17*17.

Non-prime numbers are called **composite** numbers. Prime numbers provide for composite numbers as the elements of the periodic table provide for chemical compounds.

The Greek mathematician, Eratosthenes, devised a method for generating a list of the prime numbers less than 100. Eratosthenes' method is called a **sieve.** It starts with a list of consecutive numbers beginning with the number 2.

	2	3	4	5	6	7	8	9	10
11	12	13	14	15	16	17	18	19	20
21	22	23	24	25	26	27	28	29	30
31	32	33	34	35	36	37	38	39	40
41	42	43	44	45	46	47	48	49	50
51	52	53	54	55	56	57	58	59	60
61	62	63	64	65	66	67	68	69	70
71	72	73	74	75	76	77	78	79	80
81	82	83	84	85	86	87	88	89	90
91	92	93	94	95	96	97	98	99	100

You first eliminate 4 and all larger multiples of 2.

2	3	5	7	9
11	13	15	17	19
21	23	25	27	29
31	33	35	37	39
41	43	45	47	49
51	53	55	57	59
61	63	65	67	69
71	73	75	77	79
81	83	85	87	89
91	93	95	97	99

You then eliminate 9 and all larger multiples of 3.

2	3	5	7	
11	13		17	19
	23	25		29
31		35	37	
41	43		47	49
	53	55		59
61		65	67	
71	73		77	79
	83	85		89
91		95	97	

You then eliminate 25 and all larger multiples of 5.

2	3	5	7
11	13		17 19
	23		29
31		37	
41	43	47	49
	53		59
61		67	
71	73	77	79
	83		89
91		97	

Finally, you eliminate 49 and all larger multiples of 7.

2	3	5	7
11	13	17	19
	23		29
31		37	
41	43	47	
	53		59
61		67	
71	73		79
	83		89
		97	

The remaining twenty-five numbers are **prime numbers**.

The challenge is to write a **Python** program that will determine if a given number, N, is a prime number. The **Python** code is shown below:

```
""" The program determines if n is a prime number.
"""

n = int(input('Enter a number: '))
if n > 1:
    for j in range(2, n):
        if n % j == 0:
            print (n, 'is a multiple of', j)
            print ('so', n, 'is not a prime number.')
            break
    else:
        print (n, 'is a prime number.')
```

. . .

Several executions of the program are shown below:

```
Enter a number: 1591
1591 is a multiple of 37
so 1591 is not a prime number.

Enter a number: 1593
1593 is a multiple of 3
so 1593 is not a prime number.

Enter a number: 1597
1597 is a prime number.
```

Every prime number other than 2 is an odd number. There is a lengthy method for finding the **first prime number** after a **given number**.

For example, to find the first prime number after 140, start with 141 and use division to discover 3 is a factor of 141, so 141 is not a prime number.

Add 2 to 141 for 143 and use division to discover that neither 3 nor 7 is a factor of 143, but that 11 is a factor of 143, so 143 is not a prime number.

Add 2 to 143 for 145 and use division to discover 3 is not a factor of 145, but that 5 is a factor of 145, so 145 is not a prime number.

Add 2 to 145 for 147 and use division to discover 3 is a factor of 147, so 147 is not a prime number.

Add 2 to 147 for 149 and use division to discover that neither 3, nor 5, nor 7, nor 11 are factors of 149.

Therefore, 149 is the first prime number after 140.

. . .

You might ask why I didn't check to see if 13 and other larger prime numbers are factors of 149. I didn't need to because **divisors** of a number, also called **factors** of a number, come in **pairs**. Pairs of factors of a number can be equal, as in the case of 144 = 12 * 12. Otherwise, one factor of the pair will be larger than the other factor.

For example, 120 can be expressed as 2 * 60, or 3 * 40, or 5 * 24, or 6 * 20 or 10 * 12. The smaller factors, 2, 3, 5, 6 and 10 are all smaller than the larger corresponding factors 60, 40, 24, 20 and 12. In fact, the smaller factors are each smaller than 11, while the corresponding larger factors are each larger than 11.

Given a number A, the number B separating the small factors of A from the large factors of A is the square root of A, rounded to the nearest whole number.

The square root of 149 is approximately 12.207, so I didn't need to check whether 13 is a factor of 149, because 13 is larger than 12.

. . .

The method described above would be **very lengthy** for a large number. For this reason, computers are used to find prime numbers.

The challenge is to write a **Python** program to calculate and display the prime number between two given numbers, inclusive of the two numbers. The code for the program is shown below.

```
""" The program determines and displays the prime numbers
between n and m, inclusive of n and m. """

n = int(input('Enter a beginning number: '))
m = int(input('Enter an ending number: '))
primes = []
for p_p in range(n, m + 1):
    TorF = True
    for j in range(2, p_p):
        if p_p % j == 0:
            TorF = False
            break
    if TorF:
        primes.append(p_p)
print ('There are', len(primes), 'prime numbers between', n, 'and', m)
print ('They are shown below.')
print (primes)
```

. . .

Three executions of the program are shown below:

Enter a beginning number: 10
Enter an ending number: 20
There are 4 prime numbers between 10 and 20
They are shown below.
[11, 13, 17, 19]

Enter a beginning number: 100
Enter an ending number: 200
There are 21 prime numbers between 100 and 200
They are shown below.
[101, 103, 107, 109, 113, 127, 131, 137, 139, 149, 151, 157, 163, 167, 173, 179, 181, 191, 193, 197, 199]

Enter a beginning number: 500
Enter an ending number: 1000
There are 73 prime numbers between 500 and 1000
They are shown below.
[503, 509, 521, 523, 541, 547, 557, 563, 569, 571, 577, 587, 593, 599, 601, 607, 613, 617, 619, 631, 641, 643, 647, 653, 659, 661, 673, 677, 683, 691, 701, 709, 719, 727, 733, 739, 743, 751, 757, 761, 769, 773, 787, 797, 809, 811, 821, 823, 827, 829, 839, 853, 857, 859, 863, 877, 881, 883, 887, 907, 911, 919, 929, 937, 941, 947, 953, 967, 971, 977, 983, 991, 997]

. . .

4.2 Euclid's Perfect-Prime Theorem

Euclid lived some three years after the Pythagoreans. In addition to his **Perfect-Prime Theorem,** he proved that there is no largest prime number. This proof is considered one of the most beautiful in all of mathematics. With no largest prime number, the collection of prime numbers is infinite.

Some three hundred years before Euclid, the Pythagoreans, with their mystical and religious view of numbers, defined a number to be **perfect** if it was equal to the sum of its proper divisors. Euclid was also interested in perfect numbers and studied the powers of 2 as a possible source of perfect numbers. A power of 2 has only one prime divisor, making it easy to determine all of its proper divisors.

Euclid discovered and proved:

If $2^P - 1$ is a prime number, then $(2^P - 1) * 2^{(P-1)}$ is a perfect number.

For the prime number 3, we have $3 = 2^2 - 1$ and $(2^2 - 1) * 2^{(2-1)} = 3 * 2 = 6$, a perfect number (see Section 3.2).

For the prime number 7, we have $7 = 2^3 - 1$ and $(2^3 - 1) * 2^{(3-1)} = 7 * 4 = 28$, a perfect number.

For the prime number 31, we have $31 = 2^5 - 1$ and $(2^5 - 1) * 2^{(5-1)} = 31 * 16 = 496$, a perfect number.

For the prime number 127, we have $127 = 2^7 - 1$ and $(2^7 - 1) * 2^{(7-1)} = 127 * 64 = 8{,}128$. The number 8,128 is a multiple of $64 = 2^6$, so 1, 2, 4, 8, 16, 32 and 64 are proper divisors of 8,128.

Using the formula $\mathbf{2^0 + 2^1 + 2^2 + 2^3 + \cdots + 2^N = 2^{N+1} - 1}$, from Section 3.2, the sum, $(1 + 2 + 2^2 + 2^3 + 2^4 + 2^5)$ equals $2^6 - 1$, or 63.

The prime number 127 is the only other divisor of 8,128, where 8128 = 64*127. So, the other proper divisors of 8,128 are the six products: 1 * 127, 2 * 127, 4 * 127, 8 * 127, 16 * 127 and 32 * 127. The sum of these six products equals $127 * (1 + 2 + 2^2 + 2^3 + 2^4 + 2^5)$, or $127 * (2^6 - 1)$, or 127 * 63.

The thirteen proper divisors of 8,128 are 1, 2, 4, 8, 16, 32, 64 and 1 * 127, 2 * 127, 4 * 127, 8 * 127, 16 * 127 and 32 * 127. The sum of all thirteen proper divisors equals 63 + 127 * 63 or 64 * 127, or 8,128. So, 8,128 is a perfect number.

Euclid knew of only the first four perfect numbers: 6, 28, 496 and 8,128; yet his theorem **promised** there are more. The next perfect number was found long after Euclid's time. The prime number 8,191, which equals $2^{13} - 1$, was used to determine the fifth perfect number. It is equal to $(2^{13} - 1)(2^{(13-1)})$, or 33,550,336.

. . .

Two theorems regarding prime numbers are stated below:

If P and Q are twin primes, then one plus their product is a number squared.

If P and Q are twin primes, where Q = P + 2, then for some number N, Q = 6N + 1 and P = 6N − 1.

See **Appendix A** for a discussion and proofs of these two theorems.

4.2 Decomposing Composite Numbers

Each composite number can be expressed in terms of multiplication and its prime divisors. Such an expression is called the **prime-decomposition of a number**. For example, the **prime-decomposition** of 100 is 2 * 2 * 5 * 5.

The challenge is to write a **Python** program that will decompose a given number into the product of its prime divisors. Given a number N, the strategy is to break the rocess into four steps.

Step 1 – Create a list of the prime divisors of N.
Step 2 – For the prime divisors that divide N more than once, add more to the list of prime divisors.
Step 3 - Sort the list from smallest to largest.
Step 4 – Create a string of the prime divisors to display the prime decomposition of N.

For example, given the composite number 1,350, the list of prime divisors will first be equal to [2, 3, 5] (1,350 = 2 * 675, 1,350 = 3 * 3 * 3 * 50 and 1,350 = 5 * 5 * 54.) So, the sorted list will contain [2, 3, 3, 3, 5, 5].

The string used to display the answer will be equal to 2 * 3 * 3 * 3 * 5 * 5.

See the code for the **Python** program below and on the next page.

```
""" Program decomposes a given number into a product of
its prime divisors.
"""

def is_it_prime(m):
    T = True
    if m > 1:
        for j in range(2, m):
            if m % j == 0:
                T = False
                break
    return T

# Main program:
n = int(input('Enter a number to be decomposed: '))
divisors = []
div_str = ''

for j in range(2, n):        # Create the list of
    if n % j == 0 and j < n:  # prime divisors of n.
        T = is_it_prime(j)
        if T:
            divisors.append(j)
```

```python
# Create a list of prime divisors
# that divide n more than once.
for j in range(len(divisors)):
    power = 2
    p = n % divisors[j]**power
    while p == 0:
        divisors.append(divisors[j])
        power = power + 1
        p = n % divisors[j]**power
divisors.sort()

for j in range(len(divisors) - 1):
    p = str(divisors[0]) + ' * '
    div_str = div_str + p
    divisors.remove(divisors[0])
if len(divisors) != 0:
    d = divisors[0]
    p = str(divisors[0])
    div_str = div_str + p
    print ('The prime decomposition of', n, 'is', div_str)
else:
    print (n, 'is a prime number')
```

. . .

Several executions of the program are shown below.

Enter a number to be decomposed: 126
The prime decomposition of 126 is 2 * 3 * 3 * 7

Enter a number to be decomposed: 3185
The prime decomposition of 3185 is 5 * 7 * 7 * 13

Enter a number to be decomposed: 28611
The prime decomposition of 28611 is 3 * 3 * 11 * 17 * 17

Enter a number to be decomposed: 1024
The prime decomposition of 1024 is
2 * 2 * 2 * 2 * 2 * 2 * 2 * 2 * 2 * 2

. . .

4.3 The Distribution of Prime Numbers

To understand how the prime numbers are distributed among all the counting numbers, mathematicians have studied the size of the gaps between prime numbers. By the size of a gap we mean the number of consecutive composite numbers between two prime numbers.

For example, the seven consecutive composite numbers 90, 91, 92, 93, 94, 95 and 96 are between the prime numbers 89 and 97, so the gap-size between 89 and 97 is seven (7). Twin primes such as 3 and 5, 5 and 7, 11 and 13 as well as 17 and 19 have a gap-size of one (1).

Gap-sizes can be arbitrarily large, as revealed by the following theorem:

For every number N, there is at least one pair of prime numbers, P and Q, with at least N consecutive composite numbers between P and Q.

In Section 4.1, I wrote a Python program that calculated and displayed the prime numbers between two given numbers. I am now challenged to write a Python program that calculates and displays the composite numbers after a given prime numbers and before the next prime number.

Shown below is the code for the program.

```
""" Program, composites_between, calculates and displays
the composite numbers between a given prime number
and the next prime number.
"""


def is_it_prime(m):
    T = True
    if m > 1:
        for j in range(2, m):
            if m % j == 0:
                T = False
                break
    return T


def next_prime(p):
    T = False
    j = p + 2
    while T == False:
        T = is_it_prime(j)
        if T:
            break
        else:
            j = j + 2
    return j
```

```
# Main program:
n = int(input('Enter a prime number: '))
T = is_it_prime(n)
if T:
    composites = [1]
    m = next_prime(n)
    for j in range(n + 1, m):
        for k in range(2, 97):
            if j % k == 0 and j not in composites:
                composites.append(j)
    composites.remove(1)
    print ('There are', len(composites), 'composite numbers
between',n,'and',m)
    print ('They are', composites)
else:
    print (n, 'is not a prime number.')
```

. . .

Several executions of the program are shown below:

Enter a prime number: 23
There are 5 composite numbers between 23 and 29
They are [24, 25, 26, 27, 28]

Enter a prime number: 719
There are 7 composite numbers between 719 and 727
They are [720, 721, 722, 723, 724, 725, 726]

Enter a prime number: 1327
There are 33 composite numbers between 1327 and 1361
They are [1328, 1329, 1330, 1331, 1332, 1333, 1334, 1335, 1336, 1337, 1338, 1339, 1340, 1341, 1342, 1343, 1344, 1345, 1346, 1347, 1348, 1349, 1350, 1351, 1352, 1353, 1354, 1355, 1356, 1357, 1358, 1359, 1360]

. . .

I could use the 'composites_between' program to search for prime numbers with a given gap-size, but there is a **formulated procedure** that will more directly produce two prime numbers with a gap-size of at least N. The formulation uses the mathematical function N-factorial.

N-factorial is abbreviated as 'N!' and is defined as the **product** of the consecutive numbers from 1 to N, i.e., 1 * 2 * 3 *...* (N - 2) * (N - 1) * N. For example, by definition 6! = 1 * 2 * 3 * 4 * 5 * 6, or 720.

Consider the sequence of these five consecutive numbers [6! + 2], [6! + 3], [6! + 4], [6! + 5], [6! + 6]. These five consecutive numbers are multiples of 2, 3, 4, 5 and 6, respectively. Therefore, each is a composite number.

For example, 6! + 4 = 1 * 2 * 3 * 4 * 5 * 6 + 4 = 4 * (1 + 1 * 2 * 3 * 5 * 6).

The five consecutive composite numbers, [6! + 2], [6! + 3], [6! + 4], [6! + 5], [6! + 6], have values 722, 723, 724, 725 and 726, respectively. They are each between the prime numbers 719 and 727. We now have the seven composite numbers 720, 721, 722, 723, 724, 725 and 726 between the prime numbers 719 and 727 (e.g., 721 = 7 * 103.), so the gap- size between 719 and 727 is seven.

The formulation:

$[(N + 1)! + 2], [(N + 1)! + 3], \ldots [(N + 1)! + (N + 1)]$

will produce N consecutive numbers and will be used in a Python program further on. As in the example above, these N numbers are multiples of 2, 3, 4, ..., (N + 1), respectively.

I will need a **Python** program to calculate the factorial of numbers, i.e., N!. See the code of the program below.

```
""" The function, factorial(), returns
n!, or 1 * 2 * 3 * 4 * ... * n.
"""


def factorial(n):
    p = 1
    for j in range(2, n + 1):
        p = p * j
    print (n, '- factorial equals',  p)
```

. . .

Several executions of the program are shown on the next page:

```
>>> factorial(1)
1 - factorial equals 1
>>> factorial(2)
2 - factorial equals 2
>>> factorial(3)
3 - factorial equals 6
>>> factorial(4)
4 - factorial equals 24
>>> factorial(5)
5 - factorial equals 120
>>> factorial(6)
6 - factorial equals 720
>>> factorial(7)
7 - factorial equals 5040
>>> factorial(8)
8 - factorial equals 40320
>>> factorial(9)
9 - factorial equals 362880
>>> factorial(10)
10 - factorial equals 3628800
>>> factorial(50)
50 - factorial equals
30414093201713378043612608166064768844377641568
96051200000000000
```

We see that for even small numbers, N-factorial produces very large numbers.

. . .

The challenge is to write a Python program that will use the formulation,
[(N + 1)! + 2], [(N + 1)! + 3], [(N + 1)! + 4] ... [(N + 1)! + (N + 1)],
to produce two prime numbers with a gap size of N.

The program will first create a list of $N - 1$ consecutive numbers from [(N + 1)! + 2] to [(N + 1)! + (N + 1)]. The program will extend this list downward to first prime number smaller than [(N + 1)! + 2]. It will then extend the list upward to the first prime number after [(N + 1)! + (N + 1)].

For example, given N = 5, [(5 + 1)! + 2] equals 122, the original list will be [122, 123, 124, 125].
This list will be extended downward to 113 and upward to 127. The sorted list will be:
[113, 114, 115, 116, 117, 118, 120, 121, 122, 123, 124, 125, 126, 127].

We will then have twelve consecutive composite numbers between the prime numbers 113 and 127.

The Python code for the program is shown below and on the next page.

""" The program, N_Consecutive_Composites() determines the first two prime numbers with at least N consecutive composite numbers between the two prime numbers.
"""

```python
def is_it_prime(n):
    T = True
    for j in range(2, n):
        if n % j == 0:
            T = False
    return T

def previous_prime(p):
    global terms
    T_F = False
    j = p - 1
    while T_F == False:
        T = is_it_prime(j)
        if T:
            break
        else:
            terms.append(j)
            j = j - 1
    return j
```

```python
def next_prime(p):
    global terms
    T_F = False
    j = p + 1
    while T_F == False:
        T = is_it_prime(j)
        if T:
            break
        else:
            terms.append(j)
            j = j + 1
    return j

def factorial(f):
    product = 1
    for j in range(2, f + 1):
        product = product * j
    return product

# Main program:
global terms
n = int(input('Enter the quantity of composite numbers: '))
print('')
terms = []
fctor = factorial(n)
```

```
for j in range(2, n + 1):
    n = j + fctor
    terms.append(n)

first_prime = previous_prime(terms[0])
terms.sort()
Length = len(terms)
last_prime = next_prime(terms[Length - 1])
terms.sort()
print('There are', Length, 'composite numbers')
print('between', first_prime, 'and', last_prime)
```

. . .

Several executions of the program are shown below and on the next page.

Enter the quantity of composite numbers: 4

There are 5 composite numbers
between 23 and 29

Enter the quantity of composite numbers: 5

There are 12 composite numbers
between 113 and 127

Enter the quantity of composite numbers: 6

There are 7 composite numbers
between 719 and 727

Enter the quantity of composite numbers: 7

There are 8 composite numbers
between 5039 and 5051

Enter the quantity of composite numbers: 8

There are 39 composite numbers
between 40289 and 40343

Enter the quantity of composite numbers: 9

There are 22 composite numbers
between 362867 and 362897

Enter the quantity of composite numbers: 10

There are 21 composite numbers
between 3628789 and 3628811

WARNING! Entering a quantity larger than 10 will
require several minutes, or even hours to return a result.

. . .

In spite of the existence of large gaps between prime numbers, guaranteed by the theorem:

For every number N, there is at least one pair of prime numbers, P and Q, with at least N consecutive composite numbers between P and Q.

there is another, seemingly contradictory, theorem:

For every number N, larger than 1, there is at least one prime number between N and 2N.

This second theorem began as a conjecture proposed by Joseph Bertrand (1822 – 1900). It was first proven in 1850 by Pafnuty Chebyshev (1821 – 1894). At the age of 19, **Paul Erdos** (1913 – 1996), provided a much more elegant proof of the theorem.

Considering both theorems leads to a corollary:
In a list of composite numbers between a prime number N and the next prime number Q, twice the number N+1 will be larger than Q.

For example, in the list of 53 composite numbers between 40289 and 40343, twice 40290 equals 80580, which is larger than 40343.

. . .

Chapter Five: Some Ancient Mathematics

5.1 Euclid's Algorithm for GCD

As Euclid explored numbers, he needed a method to determine when two numbers are **relatively-prime.** Two numbers are **relatively-prime** if the number 1 is their only common divisor. To this end, Euclid created a procedure to find the largest common divisor of two given numbers. This number is called the **Greatest Common Divisor**, or **GCD,** of the two given numbers. If the GCD of two numbers is the number 1, then the two numbers are relatively prime.

Euclid's method for finding the GCD of 3,927 and 255 proceeds as follows:

Divide 3,927 by 255 for a quotient of 15 and remainder 102.

Then divide the previous divisor, 255, by the previous remainder, 102, for a quotient of 2 and remainder 51.

Then divide the previous divisor, 102, by the previous remainder, 51, for a quotient of 2 and remainder 0.

The last division resulted in a zero remainder, so the GCD of 3,927 and 255 is the previous remainder, 51.

It is natural to ask: How did Euclid determine quotients and remainders? He probably used **subtraction**. For example, to determine the quotient of 28 divided by 7, he could **count** the number of times 7 can be **subtracted** from 28 before arriving at 0. The **count**, 4, would be his quotient.

To determine the quotient of 30 divided by 7, he could count the number of times 7 can be subtracted from 30 before arriving at **a number less than** 7. The **count**, 4, would be his **quotient** and the **left-over, 2,** would be his remainder.

Today, when was using a simple hand-held calculator to determine the quotient when 97 is divided by 13, I would enter 97/13 for the result 7.46153846. The number 7 before the decimal point is the quotient.

Subtracting 7 from 7.46153846 results in the decimal number .46153846. Multiplying this decimal number by the divisor, 13, provides the remainder 6.

• • •

Euclid's procedure for finding the **GCD** of two numbers is called **Euclid's Algorithm.** One has to wonder how Euclid discovered it. In Euclid's time, there were no decimal numbers, only fractions, so **perhaps** he would have expressed $\frac{3927}{255}$ as $15 + \frac{102}{255}$.

With $\frac{3{,}927}{255}$ as $15 + \frac{102}{255}$, Euclid could then express $\frac{3{,}927}{255}$ as $15 + \frac{2*51}{5*51}$, then as $15 + \frac{2}{5}$ then as $\frac{77}{5}$.

With $\frac{3{,}927}{255}$ as $\frac{77}{5}$, Euclid would have

$$3{,}927 = \frac{77*255}{5} = \mathbf{77 * 51}.$$

Euclid could then express $\frac{255}{102}$ as $2 + \frac{51}{102}$,

then as $2 + \frac{1}{2}$, or $\frac{5}{2}$.

With $\frac{255}{102} = \frac{5}{2}$, Euclid would have $255 = \frac{5*102}{2}$, or

5 * 51.

With $3{,}927 = \mathbf{77 * 51}$ and $255 = \mathbf{5 * 51}$, Euclid would conclude the GCD of 3,927 and 255 is **51**.

. . .

113

I used my internet browser to discover the code other **Python** programmers wrote to calculate the GCD of two numbers. I found the following:

```python
def gcd(x, y):
    while y != 0:
        (x, y) = (y, x % y)
    return x
```

The programmer gave Euclid credit but failed to discuss why Euclid's Algorithm works. I wanted to write a Python program that used the definition of the GCD.

My challenge is to write a **Python** program that **demonstrates** the step of Euclid's Algorithms. The program code is shown below.

```python
""" The program executes Euclid's Algorithm to
calculate the GREATEST COMMON DIVISOR of two
numbers.
"""

n = int(input('Enter a number greater than 1: '))
m = int(input('Enter a larger number: '))
Dividend = m
Divisor = n
R = m % n
Q = int(m / n)
```

```
print (Dividend, 'is the dividend.')
print (Divisor, 'is the divisor.')
print (R, 'is the remainder.')
print ('')
while Divisor > 0:
        Dividend = Divisor
        Divisor = R
        if R > 0:
                Q = int(Dividend / Divisor)
                R = Dividend % Divisor
                print (Dividend, 'is the new dividend.')
                print (Divisor, 'is the new divisor.')
                print (Q, 'is the quotient')
                print (R, 'is the remainder.')
                print ('')

if Dividend == 1:
        print (n, 'and', m, 'are relatively-prime')
else:
        print ('GCD of ', n, 'and', m, 'is', Dividend)
```

. . .

Executions of the program is shown below:

Enter a number greater than 1: 255
Enter a larger number: 3927
3927 is the dividend.
255 is the divisor.
102 is the remainder.

255 is the new dividend.
102 is the new divisor.
2 is the quotient
51 is the remainder.

102 is the new dividend.
51 is the new divisor.
2 is the quotient
0 is the remainder.

GCD of 255 and 3927 is 51

. . .

5.2 Fermat's Two Types of Prime Numbers

Born in 1607, Pierre de Fermat graduated in 1626 with a bachelor degree in civil law from the University of Orleans, France. Even though his formal education was in law, Fermat had a deeper interest in mathematics, publishing his first mathematics paper in 1629. In 1630, he joined the legal staff at the Parliament of Toulouse, France, remaining in a high position there for the rest of his life.

Fermat spent a lot of time thinking about prime numbers. He had a deep desire to discover a formula that would represent all prime numbers. All but one prime number (2) is odd, so it was natural for Fermat to explore odd numbers.

Fermat could represent the odd numbers in terms of the number 2 (i.e., 1 plus a multiple of 2.)

Examples are:
$3 = 2 * 1 + 1$. $5 = 2 * 2 + 1$. $7 = 2 * 3 + 1$. $9 = 2 * 4 + 1$.

But Fermat determined he could also represent all odd numbers other than 3 in terms of the number 4.

Examples are:
$5 = 4 * 1 + 1$. $7 = 4 * 1 + 3$. $9 = 4 * 2 + 1$.

Note that when an odd number is divided by 4, the remainders are either 1 or 3. Using this observation, Fermat determined that prime numbers were of two types:

Type-1 prime numbers are those with remainder 1 when divided by 4.

Type-3 prime numbers are those with remainder 3 when divided by 4.

Fermat then discovered and proved:

*Type-1 prime number can be expressed as **the sum of two perfect squares***.

For example, dividing the prime number 53 by 4 leaves 1 as remainder and $53 = 2^2 + 7^2$.

Given a Type-1 prime number P, Fermat guarantees $P = A^2 + B^2$ for two perfect squares. In other words, for a Type-1 prime number P and perfect square A^2, Fermat guarantees a solution for the variable B in the equation $P - A^2 = B^2$.

To solve for B, all we have to do is **repeatedly** subtract larger and larger perfect squares from P until the solution appears. For example, $409 = 4 * 102 + 1$ is a Type-1 prime number.

A demonstration of repeated subtraction follows:
$409 - 1^2 = 408$. $409 - 2^2 = 405$. $409 - 3^2 = 400$, a perfect square. So, $409 = 3^2 + 20^2$. This repeated subtraction is referred to as the **subtraction-technique.**

Each positive number N can act as a **potential generator** of a Fermat Type-1 prime number; **potential** because 4N+1 might not be a prime number.

For example, the numbers, $4 * 2 + 1 = 9$, where 9 is not a prime number, while $4 * 3 + 1 = 13$, where 13 is a prime number.

My challenge is to write a **Python** program to generate a sequence of Fermat Type-1 prime numbers along with their representation as a sum of two perfect squares.

Given a number N, the sequence will begin with an initial the number M = 4 * N + 1 and determine if M is a prime number. If M is a prime number, the program will search for two perfect squares that sum to M.

The **Python** code for the program is shown on the next page.

""" The program will express a Fermat-Type-1 prime number as the sum of two perfect squares. Starting with an initial number N, the program will form odd numbers M = 4N + 1 and determine if each M is a prime number. If M is a prime number, the program will subtract perfect squares from M, i.e., M-1^2, M-2^2, M-3^2, etc. until the result is a perfect square, S^2. With M - K^2 = S^2 the program will have found M = K^2 + S^2. """

Determine if n is a prime number.

```python
def is_it_prime(p):
    T = True
    if p > 1:
        for j in range(2, p):
            if p % j == 0:
                T = False
                break
    return T
```

Find a perfect square.
```python
def perfect_square(p):
    pair = []
    for j in range(1, 5):
        for k in range(j + 1, p - 1):
            if j**2 + k**2 == p:
                pair = [j, k]
                break
    return pair
```

```python
# Main program:

n = int(input('Enter a number: '))
print('Each number before the = is a Fermat Type-1 prime
number.')
for num in range(n, n + 30):
    M = 4 * num + 1
    T = is_it_prime(M)
    if T:
        pair = perfect_square(M)
        if pair:
            K = pair[0]
            S = pair[1]
            print(M, '=', K**2, '+', S**2)
```

. . .

An execution of the program is shown below:

Enter a number: 3
Each number before the = is a Fermat Type-1 prime
number
$13 = 4 + 9$
$17 = 1 + 16$
$29 = 4 + 25$
$37 = 1 + 36$
$41 = 16 + 25$
$53 = 4 + 49$
$73 = 9 + 64$
$97 = 16 + 81$
$101 = 1 + 100$
$109 = 9 + 100$

. . .

No Fermat Type-3 odd number can be expressed as a sum of two perfect squares. See Appendix B for a proof of this statement.

. . .

Chapter Six: Exploring Even Numbers

6.1 Jack's Procedure

Some even numbers can be expressed as the sum of consecutive numbers. Below are examples:

$6 = 1 + 2 + 3.$
$10 = 1 + 2 + 3 + 4.$
$12 = 3 + 4 + 5.$
$14 = 2 + 3 + 4 + 5.$
$18 = 3 + 4 + 5 + 6 = 5 + 6 + 7.$
$20 = 2 + 3 + 4 + 5 + 6.$
$22 = 4 + 5 + 6 + 7.$

Although powers of 2 are even numbers, none can be expressed as the sum of consecutive numbers. See Appendix C for a proof of this statement.

I devised an interactive procedure for finding the fewest consecutive numbers summing to a given even number. The sum will require at least three consecutive numbers, so the procedure starts the search at the integer-value of the even number divided by 3.

For example, if **N** = 22, then **M** = 7 (22 / 3 = 7.33…), so we determine if the sum of 7 + 8 + 9 is 22. The sum 24 so the procedure will then add and subtract specific numbers until the correct sum appears.

The initial sum, 24, is too big, so subtract 9 and add 6 for 6 + 7 + 8, or 21.

Our target is 22, while 21 is too small. Next add 5 for 5 + 6 + 7 + 8, or 26.

Our target is 22, while 26 is too large. Subtract 8 and add 4 for 4 + 5 + 6 + 7. The sum equals 22, so the procedure yields 22 = 4 + 5 + 6 + 7.

My challenge is to write a **Python** program that uses the procedure described to find the fewest consecutive numbers summing to a given even number. The code for the **Python** program is shown on the next two pages.

""" The program, Jack'S Procedure.py, produces a series of consecutive number, each summing to given even number. Given an even number E, the procedure starts with a series of three consecutive numbers with a SUM a bit less than or a bit larger than E. By adding and/or subtracting from the series the procedures arrives at a series with a SUM equal to E. The procedure works for every even number EXCEPT powers of 2.
"""

```python
def too_small(num_lst):
    num_lst.append(num_lst[0] - 1)
    return num_lst

def too_large(num_lst):
    num_lst.remove(num_lst[len(num_lst) - 1])
    num_lst.append(num_lst[0] - 1)
    return num_lst

# Main progtram:
print_str = ''
Even = int(input('Enter an even number other than a power of 2: '))
num_lst = []
First = int(Even / 3)
num_lst.append(First)
num_lst.append(First + 1)
num_lst.append(First + 2)
SUM = sum(num_lst)
```

```python
while SUM != Even:
    if SUM > Even:
        num_lst = too_large(num_lst)
    else:
        num_lst = too_small(num_lst)
    num_lst.sort()
    SUM = sum(num_lst)
for j in range(len(num_lst) - 1):
        num = num_lst[j]
        print_str = print_str + str(num) + ' + '
print_str = print_str + str(num_lst[len(num_lst) - 1])
print (print_str, ' = ', SUM)
```

. . .

Several executions of the program are shown below:

Enter an even number other than a power of 2: 96
$31 + 32 + 33 = 96$

Enter an even number other than a power of 2: 98
$23 + 24 + 25 + 26 = 98$
Enter an even number other than a power of 2: 100
$18 + 19 + 20 + 21 + 22 = 100$

Enter an even number other than a power of 2: 112
$13 + 14 + 15 + 16 + 17 + 18 + 19 = 112$

Enter an even number other than a power of 2: 116
$11 + 12 + 13 + 14 + 15 + 16 + 17 + 18 = 116$

Enter an even number other than a power of 2: 1006
$250 + 251 + 252 + 253 = 1006$

Enter an even number other than a power of 2: 1008
$335 + 336 + 337 = 1008$

Enter an even number other than a power of 2: 1010
$251 + 252 + 253 + 254 = 1010$

Enter an even number other than a power of 2: 1012
$123 + 124 + 125 + 126 + 127 + 128 + 129 + 130 = 1012$

Enter an even number other than a power of 2: 1014
$337 + 338 + 339 = 1014$

Enter an even number other than a power of 2: 30100
$6018 + 6019 + 6020 + 6021 + 6022 = 30100$

Enter an even number other than a power of 2: 44222
$11054 + 11055 + 11056 + 11057 = 44222$

Enter an even number other than a power of 2: 88666
$22165 + 22166 + 22167 + 22168 = 88666$

Enter an even number other than a power of 2: 100000
$19998 + 19999 + 20000 + 20001 + 20002 = 100000$

Enter an even number other than a power of 2: 100224
$33407 + 33408 + 33409 = 100224$

· · ·

6.2 A Trial and Error Procedure

While writing the book *Discoveries in a Playground of Numbers*, I discovered a formula for finding a series of consecutive numbers that sum to a given even number E. The formula relates the beginning number N, of the series to the length, L, of the series.

The formula is: $N = F - \dfrac{[F+(F+1)+\cdots+(F+L-1)]-E}{Lenth\ of\ [F+(F+1)+\cdots+(F+L-1)]}$,

where **E** is a given even number, **F** equal the integer-value of **E** divide by 3 and **L** represent the length of the series.

$$E = N + (N + 1) + (N + 2) + \cdots + (M - 1) + M,$$
where the last number in the series, M equal $L + N - 1$.

For example, with **E** = 112, F equals the integer-value of 112/3, or 37. Then $F + L - 1 = 37 + L - 1$.

By substituting the values 3, 4, 5, etc., for L in the formula

$N = 37 - \dfrac{[37 + 38 + \ldots + (37 + L - 1)] - 112}{L}$ would eventually reveal the combination of $N = 13$ and $L = 7$.

We would then have
$$112 = 13 + 14 + 15 + 16 + 17 + 18 + 19.$$

My challenge is to write a Python program that substitutes values for L in the formulation

$$N = F - \frac{[F+(F+1)+\cdots+(F+L-1)]-E}{Lenth \ of \ [F+(F+1)+\cdots+(F+L-1)]}$$

to find a series of consecutive numbers that sum to a given even number **E.** See the **Python** code for the program below.

""" The program, **trial_and_error.py**, uses a formula I discoverd. The formula,

N = F - ([F + (F + 1) + ⋯ + (F + L - 1)] - E) / (Length of [F + (F + 1) + ⋯ + (F + L - 1)]),

provides a trial procedure for finding the first number, N,
in a series that will sum to given even number E.
F equals the integer-value of E divided by 3,
and becomes the first possible number in the series.
"""

```
Even = int(input('Enter an even number other than a power of 2: '))
series_list = []
First = int(Even / 3)
Length_of_series = 2
sum_of_series = 0

while sum_of_series != Even:
    Length_of_series = Length_of_series + 1
    SUM = 0
```

```python
for j in range(First, First + Length_of_series):
    SUM = SUM + j
First = int(First - (SUM - Even) / Length_of_series)
Last = Length_of_series + First - 1
sum_of_series = int((Last + First) * (Last - First + 1) / 2)
Last = Length_of_series + First - 1

series_lst = []
for j in range(First, Last + 1):
    series_lst.append(str(j))
print('')
print(Even, '=', ' + '.join(series_lst))
```

. . .

Several executions of the program are shown below.

Enter an even number other than a power of 2: 96

96 = 31 + 32 + 33

Enter an even number other than a power of 2: 1006

1006 = 250 + 251 + 252 + 253

Enter an even number other than a power of 2: 1010

1010 = 251 + 252 + 253 + 254

Enter an even number other than a power of 2: 44222

44222 = 11054 + 11055 + 11056 + 11057

· · ·

The results of **trial_and_error.py** are the same as those of **Jack's procedure.py**.

· · ·

6.3 Adams' Algorithm

Laura Adams was a high school junior in one of my high school honors math classes. One day, I showed the students in her class my procedure as described in Section 6.1 I then challenged the students to find a more elegant solution. Two days later, Laura came to class and provided an original and creative procedure.

Laura went to the chalkboard and presented the following example:

*"Given the even number E = 56, I need the **largest odd divisor** of 56 and the **largest even divisor** of 56. The **largest odd divisor** is found by continually dividing 56 by 2 until no even number remains.*

*Dividing 56 by 2 equals 28. Dividing 28 by 2 equals 14. Dividing 14 by 2 equals 7. So, 7 is the **largest odd divisor** of 56 and 8 is the **largest even divisor** of 56.*

Subtract 1 from the largest odd divisor of 56 and divide the result by 2. The result is $\frac{7-1}{2}$, or 3. Compare this 3 with 8. Because 3 is less than 8, the largest even divisor of 56, the first number in the series will be 8 - 3, or 5.

We learned a formula for the sum of the numbers from N to M is $\left(\frac{N+M}{2}\right) * (M - N + 1)$. Applying this formula to N = 5 we have the equation $\left(\frac{5+M}{2}\right) * (M - 5 + 1)$ for the quadratic equation

$M^2 + M - 132 = 0$. This equation factors to $(M + 12)(M - 11) = 0$. So, M = 11.
The series begins with N = 5 and ends with M = 11, so 56 = 5+6+7+8+9+10+11."

Although none of us understood how Laura came up with her procedure, Laura received a loud applause from the class.

Laura's procedure was straight forward, requiring no trial-and-error searching, nor any logical decision making. If one substitutes numbers into her formulation the way Laura described, then one should get a correct series.

A precise formulation of Laura's procedure is described below:

Given an even number, **E,** other than a power of 2, let **D** be the **largest odd divisor** of **E,** and let **Q** be the result of dividing **E** by **D**. **Q** will be the **largest even divisor** of E, and **Q** will be a power of 2.

Let $L = (D - 1)$ divided by 2. **D** is an odd number, so $D - 1$ is an even number. Therefore, **L** will always be a whole number.

Let **N** represent the first number in a series that sums to the given even number **E**. If Q > L, then **N,** the first number will be equal to **Q – L**, otherwise, the first number will be equal to **L – Q + 1**.

The last number will be the solution to the equation:
$$\left(\frac{N + M}{2}\right) * (M - N + 1) = E$$ for the variable **M**.

. . .

I decided to call Laura's procedure Adams' Algorithm. My challenge was to write a **Python** program that used Adams' Algorithm to find a series of consecutive numbers which sums to a given even number. See the **Python** code for the program on the next page.

""" The program Adams.py, finds a series that sums to a given even number. In 1977, Laura Adams was a high school student. She discovered a procedure to find the first and last numbers in a series that summed to a given even number. For the even number, E, other than a power of 2, let D be the largest odd divisor of E. Let Q = E divided by D, then Q will be the largest even divisor of E, and it will be a power of 2. Let L = (D - 1) divided by 2. L will be an even number and will be used to determine the value of the first number, N, in the series. If Q > L, then the first number will be equal to Q - L, otherwise the first number will be equal to L - Q + 1. The last number, M will be equal to the solution to the equation $\left(\frac{N+M}{2}\right) * (M - N + 1) = E$.
"""

```
Even = int(input('Enter an even number other than a power of 2: '))
series = []
Largest_odd_divisor = int(Even / 2)
remainder = Largest_odd_divisor % 2

while remainder != 1:
    Largest_odd_divisor = int(Largest_odd_divisor / 2)
    if Largest_odd_divisor == int(Largest_odd_divisor):
        remainder = Largest_odd_divisor % 2
Power_of_2 = int( Even / Largest_odd_divisor)
Decider = int(Largest_odd_divisor / 2)
if Power_of_2 > Decider:
    First = Power_of_2 - Decider
else:

    First = Decider - Power_of_2 + 1
Last = int(int(-1 + (1 + 4 * (First * (First - 1) + 2 * Even))**0.5) / 2)
 for j in range(First, Last + 1):
    series.append(str(j))
print('')
print(Even, '=', ' + '.join(series))
```

. . .

136

Several executions of the program are shown below.

>>> adams(22)
22 equals 4+5+6+7

>>> adams(76)
76 equals 6+7+8+9+10+11+12+13

>>> adams(100)
100 equals 9+10+11+12+13+14+15+16

>>> adams(2002)
2002 equals 499+500+501+502

>>> adams(3124)
3124 equals 387+388+389+390+391+392+393+394

>>> adams(4456)
4456 equals
271+272+273+274+275+276+277+278+279+280+281+282+283
+284+285+286

>>> adams(5128)
5128 equals
313+314+315+316+317+318+319+320+321+322+323+324+325
+326+327+328

>>> adams(15648)
15648 equals
213+214+215+216+217+218+219+220+221+222+223+224+225
+226+227+228+229+230+231+232+233+234+235+236+237+
238+239+240+241+242+243+244+245+246+247+248+249+250
+251+252+253+254+255+256+257+258+259+260+261+262+
263+264+265+266+267+268+269+270+271+272+273+274+275
+276

Comparing the results of Jack's procedure, Section 6.1 with Adams' Algorithm, Jack's procedure always provides the shortest series while sometime the series from Adams' are much longer. The code for Adams' is much shorter.

. . .

6.4 Goldbach's Conjecture

A conjecture in arithmetic is a statement about a collection of numbers that appears to be true, yet remains unproven. There are many conjectures regarding arithmetic. A conjecture is a guess that can be refuted with only one counter-example.

Christian Goldbach (1690 - 1764) was a German mathematician born in Konigsberg, a part of Prussia. In 1742, while working at the Russian Ministry of Foreign Affairs in St. Petersburg, Russia, he discovered a now famous conjecture regarding a relationship between even numbers and prime numbers.

In a letter to Euler, Goldbach wrote that he believed:

Every even number greater than 6 can be expressed as the sum of two different primes.

Some examples are:
$8 = 3 + 5.$ $10 = 3 + 7.$ $36 = 13 + 23.$
$88 = 41 + 47.$ $98 = 19 + 79.$

Goldbach's Conjecture is one of the most simply stated, yet unproven statements regarding whole numbers.

My challenge was to write a **Python** program that provides pairs of prime numbers, where each pair sums to a given even number.

Below is a description of my process:

Given an even number E, the program will create a list consisting of the prime numbers less than E. For each prime number P in this list, the program will determine if E - P is a prime number. If it is, then E - P equals some prime number Q, so E = P + Q. As a result of E = P + Q, the program will place the pair [P, Q] in the list of all such pairs.

For example, given the even number 22, the list of prime numbers less than 22 is [2, 3, 5, 7, 11, 13, 17, 19]. The numbers 22 − 2, 22 − 3, 22 − 5, 22 − 7, 22 − 11, 22 − 13, 22 − 17, and 22 − 19 equal the corresponding numbers 20, 19, 17, 15, 11, 9, 5, 3, of which 19, 17, 11, 5 and 3 are prime numbers.

We then have 22 = 3 + 19 = 5 + 17, but not 22 = 11 + 11, because the two prime numbers must be different.

The code for the program is shown on the next two pages.

""" Goldbach's conjecture claims that every even number greater than six can be expressed as the sum of two different prime numbers. This program finds five or less pairs of prime numbers, each summing to a given even number.
"""

```python
def is_it_prime(n):
    T = True
    for j in range(2, n):
        if n % j == 0:
            T = False
    return T

# Main program:
primes = [2]
pairs = []
n = int(input('Enter a number greater than 3: '))
even = 2 * n

for j in range(2, even):
    T = is_it_prime(j)
    if T:
        primes.append(j)
```

```
for j in range(len(primes)):
    prime = primes[j]
    q = even - prime
    if q in primes:
        if prime < q and prime != q:
            pair=[prime, q]
            pairs.append(pair)
            L = min(5, len(pairs))

print(")
print (even, 'equals the sum of each pair of prime numbers
shown below')
for j in range(L):
    print (pairs[j], end=' ')
```

. . .

Several executions of the program are shown below:

Enter an even number greater than 6: 22

22 equals the sum of each pair of prime numbers shown
below
[3, 19] [5, 17]

Enter an even number greater than 6: 100

100 equals the sum of each pair of prime numbers shown
below
[3, 97] [11, 89] [17, 83] [29, 71] [41, 59]

Enter an even number greater than 6: 1024

1024 equals the sum of each pair of prime numbers shown below
[3, 1021] [5, 1019] [11, 1013] [41, 983] [47, 977]

Enter an even number greater than 6: 1234

1234 equals the sum of each pair of prime numbers shown below
[3, 1231] [5, 1229] [11, 1223] [17, 1217] [41, 1193]

. . .

Appendix A

Below is a proof of the theorem:

If P and Q are twin primes, then one plus their product is a perfect square.

If N and M are numbers, where $M - N = 2$, then $M = N + 2$. So $MN + 1 = (N + 2)N + 1 = N^2 + 2N + 1$, which factors
as $(N + 1)(N + 1)$, or $(N + 1)^2$.

Therefore $MN + 1 = (N + 1)^2$.

Applying the results above to twin primes, P and Q, where $P - Q = 2$, we have $P * Q + 1 = (Q + 1)^2$.

For an example, 29 and 31 are twin primes, where $(29 * 31 + 1) = 900$ and $(29 + 1)^2 = 900$ as well.

. . .

If P and Q are twin primes, where Q = P + 2, then for some number N, Q = 6N + 1 and P = 6N − 1.

Suppose we have twin primes P and Q, where
$Q = 6J + R$ for some number J.

The remainder R is either 0, 1, 2, 3, 4, or 5. Let's consider each, other than 1, as a possible remainder. Each of the numbers $6J + 0$, $6J + 2$, $6J + 3$ and $6J + 4$ are either a multiple of 2 or 3 or both 2 and 3, and thus not a prime number. This leaves only 1 or 5 as the remainder.

If $Q = 6J + 5$, we would have
$P = Q − 2 = (6J + 5) − 2, = 6J + 3$, a multiple of 3. Since P is a prime number, Q as $6J + 5$ is impossible, leaving 1 as the only possible remainder.

With $Q = 6N + 1$, for some number N, then
$P = Q − 2 = 6N + 1 − 2 = 6N − 1$.

For example, the numbers 149 and 151 are twin primes, where $151 = 25 * 6 + 1$ and $149 = 25 * 6 - 1$.

. . .

Appendix B

Below is a proof of the statement:

No Fermat Type-3 odd number can be expressed as the sum of two perfect squares.

Suppose there is a Fermat Type-3 odd number, $N = 4J + 3$, as well as perfect squares C^2 and D^2, where

$$N = 4J + 3 = C^2 + D^2.$$

Then $4J + 3$ is an odd number and must be the sum of an even and odd number.

If C^2 is even, then C must be even and equals 2M for some number M (see **Appendix D**).

With C^2 even, D^2 must be odd and equal to $2L + 1$ for some number L.

We would then have
$N = 4J + 3 = (2M)^2 + (2L + 1)^2$, or

$N = 4M^2 + (4L^2 + 4L + 1)$, or

$N = 4(M^2 + L^2 + L) + 1$, a Fermat Type-1 odd number.

We started with the supposition that N is a Fermat Type-3 odd number, but now we have N as a Fermat Type-1 odd number. An odd number divided by 4 can have only one remainder thus cannot be of both types. We have a contradiction and the **supposition** must be false.

. . .

Appendix C

A former student, and eventually a fellow teacher and colleague, **Marshall Ransom**, proved the following theorem:

No power of 2 is expressible as a sum of consecutive numbers.

To begin, Ransom first proved the **lemma**:

No power of 2 can have an odd divisor.

Suppose to the contrary, the odd number 2K+1 divides 2^J, then $2^J = (2K + 1) * L$ for some number L.

The number L cannot be an odd number because the even number on the left side of the equation cannot equal the product of two odd numbers on the right side of the equation.

If L is an even number, then we could divide both sides of the equation by the highest power of 2 that divides L resulting in an equation with an even number on the left side and the product of two odd numbers on the right side. For example, if $2^{10} = (2K + 1) * 2^7$, then $2K + 1 = 2^3$, an impossibility. Since L can be neither odd nor even, no such L exist, and the lemma is proved.

Now for the proof of the theorem:

No power of 2 is expressible as a sum of consecutive numbers.

Suppose for some power P of 2 equals the sum of the numbers from N to M.

We would have the equation
$2^P = N + (N + 1) + \cdots + M$, i.e., the sum of the consecutive numbers from N to M. The sum of the consecutive numbers from N to M equals $\frac{(M-N+1)(M+N)}{2}$.

With $2^P = \frac{(M-N+1)(M+N)}{2}$, multiply both sides of the equation by 2 for $2^{(P+1)} = (M - N + 1)*(M + N)$.

From Ransom's **lemma** both $(M - N + 1)$ and $(M + N)$ are powers of 2.

With $M + N = 2^J$, a power of 2,
then $M - N = 2^J - 2N$.

With $M - N = 2^J - 2N$, we have
$(M - N + 1) = 2^J - 2N + 1$. We cannot have
$(M - N + 1)$ as both an odd number and a power of 2.
Therefore, the **supposition** must be false.

$\cdots$

150

Appendix D

A Note and an Example Regarding Logic

Many mathematical theorems are of the form:
If the statement P is true, then the statement Q is true.

Such forms are abbreviated as *If P, then Q.*
We also have other forms:
If not P, then Q.
If not P, then not Q.
If not Q, then not P.

The form "*If not Q, then not P*" is called the **contrapositive** of the form "*If P, then Q*".

Consider the theorem:
If the number E^2 is an even number, then the number E is an even number.

The contrapositive of the theorem is:
If the number E is an odd number, then the number E^2 is an odd number.

Since the product of two odd numbers is an odd number, the truth of the contrapositive implies the truth of the theorem.

. . .

References

Men of Mathematics, by E. T. Bell, 1937, Simon & Schuster

Mathematical Mysteries, by Calvin C. Clawson, 1996, Basic Books

Elementary Number Theory, by Gareth A. Jones and J. Mary Jones, 1998, Springer-Verlag

The Man Who Loved Only Numbers, by Paul Hoffman, 1999, Hyperion Books

A History of Mathematics, by Uta C. Merzbach and Carl B. Boyer, Third edition, 2011, John Wiley & Sons, Inc.

Love & Math, by Edward Frenkel, 2014, Basic Books

Python Without Fear, by Brian Overland, 2018, Addison-Wesley

About the Author

Jack McCabe earned a Bachelor in Math at Florida State University, a Masters in Math at Rutgers University and studied two years in a PhD program in Math at SUNY Buffalo, in New York. He served four years as an Assistant Professor of Mathematics at Stetson University in DeLand, Florida.

In Volusia County, Florida, Jack served ten years as teacher and Head of Math at Mainland High School. He then served as the Volusia School District Supervisor of Math and Testing. Jack ended his public-school career, serving three years as Assistant Principal at Deltona High School. Jack then became a New England prep school teacher, serving nineteen years as teacher and Head of Math at Canterbury School in New Milford, Connecticut.

During his teaching career, Jack helped hundreds of individual students with their math studies, resulting in Jack developing a passion for sharing his mathematical insights with others. This need to share math inspired Jack to publish this math book, as well as:

Numbers Galore: Perfects, Primes, Triples and Twins, 2013, Outskirts Press
Preparing for Calculus, 2017, Kindle Direct Publishing
Discoveries in a Playground of Numbers, 2019, Kindle Direct Publishing

And a memoir:
Unspoken Love: An Orphan's Journey, 2016, Page Publishing, Inc.

www.ingramcontent.com/pod-product-compliance
Lightning Source LLC
Chambersburg PA
CBHW080420060326
40689CB00019B/4318